MW00565445

"*LEARNING TO WALK IN FREEDOM* is just what it says—a guide to freedom. This book says more in its 80 pages than dozens of larger books I've read on the subject. It's practical, field-tested, biblical and Spirit-taught. After working for over 20 years with sexually broken people I can heartily recommend this powerful little resource!"

> **Russell Willingham**, Director of New Creation Ministries and author of *Breaking Free: Understanding Sexual Addiction and the Healing Power of Jesus* and *Relational Masks*

"Jesus said in John 8:36, 'So if the Son sets you free, you are truly free.' That verse always gets a great reaction because we all desire to truly walk in freedom! Through 24 years of ministry and 40 years as a Christian I have observed that most Christians struggle to walk in the true freedom that Christ has made possible for us. In this book, Brenna Kate Simonds lays out five insightful and powerful points that will help any Christian experience and walk in true freedom. I wish I had read this book earlier in my Christian life. It would have saved me years of wondering if I would ever be able to please God. I strongly recommend this book for any believer at any stage in their spiritual journey."

> **Pastor Jeff Jacob**, Senior Pastor, Word of Life International Church, Ashburn, Virginia

"Brenna Kate makes it easy and approachable. It makes sense that her writing would be like her personality. With clarity and honesty, Brenna Kate shares both experience and truth providing an easily understood and easily followed path in the process of living in Freedom."

> **Bob Hamp**, LMFT, Author of *Think Differently Live Differently* and Executive Pastor of Pastoral Care at Gateway Church, Southlake, TX

Learning to Walk in Freedom

A Journey in Five Steps

BRENNA KATE SIMONDS

Learning to Walk in Freedom
© 2012 by Brenna Kate Simonds
ISBN: 978-0-9911366-1-2

Copyediting and proofreading services by Carl Nellis

Cover design, and typesetting by Rusty Kinnunen, www.rustyandingrid.com

CONTENTS

FOREWORD
Mike Olejarz

Mike Olejarz was my first campus pastor back when I became a Christian in January of 1999. He's always been one of my primary mentors, did the pre-marital counseling for my husband and me, and even officiated our wedding ceremony. Since then, we've done much ministry together. I consider him both a mentor and a friend. I can't even count the ways he has positively influenced my life! Thanks for your words here, and even more so for your life, Big O. You're an example to many.

I REMEMBER an old story about two monks, an old and a young one, sent out on a mission. Their assignment was to stay together, share the message of Jesus, care for others, and return when their work was done. When they got to their assigned city of service, the younger one said they should split up to broaden their influence. The older man begrudgingly agreed, and they decided to regroup in that same spot on the city perimeter in several days.

At the appointed time, the older man arrived and waited. Two days later, he set out to locate his younger friend and found him in a six foot deep hole in the ground. He called out his name and asked, "How are you, my brother, and why are you in that hole?"

The younger man answered, "I let God, you, and the whole community down by my sinful actions. I am so ashamed. I dug this hole to hide in so I would not have to face anyone."

Then the older man said, "Step back," and jumped down into the hole with his young companion.

"Why did you do that?" the younger man asked. "Now we're both stuck!"

The older man raised his hand and replied, "Nonsense, I have been in such a spot before and know how to get out."

I met Brenna Kate Simonds when she was a college student, shortly after she decided to become a follower of Jesus. I have watched her grow and mature on her path to freedom, participated with her in iron-sharpening-iron friendship, and been grateful for her journey of discovery.

It is a joy to recommend this book. The lessons, stories, and insights she shares are fresh water to us, regardless of the particular path or station of life we find ourselves in. Like the older man in the story, she jumps into the hole we tend to dig for ourselves and shows us the way to freedom.

Brenna describes some of the giants we face, like David faced Goliath: giants of sexual attraction, eating disorders, broken identity, selfishness, and self-hate. Some days we will have difficulty. But she goes on to declare that growth, progress, and victory are possible with God's help. She clearly gives us five smooth stones, which are ammunition to win the battles we'll face.

Mike Olejarz

PREFACE
My Story

FREEDOM IS MY ANTHEM—it has been my life's theme. The questions that come with the word *freedom* are questions I continually ponder. The answers did not come easily.

I became a Christian at age 23. I came to Jesus with a lot of problems: an eating disorder, same-sex attraction, emotional dependency, self-injury, self-loathing, and chronic low self-esteem.

My life was controlled by and revolved around my issues and trying to get rid of them.

I felt like I was drowning.

Why, if I had become a new creation in Jesus (2 Corinthians 5:17), did my life not feel all that changed? Why was I still dealing with the same issues? I had a crowd of people continually praying for me. I fasted for long periods of time. I devoured the Word of God and prayed my heart out, including interceding for complete strangers whose prayer requests I found on the Internet! I went to church, led Bible studies, and sang on the worship team. I was writing songs for God and serving Him every way I knew how.

And I was still drowning.

I did gradually see the issues I struggled with loosen their external grip. I wasn't having sex with women. I wasn't starving myself or cutting. I wasn't acting out, but I didn't feel free—at all. New issues popped up—internal issues that were far more insidious than those related to acting out. Self-loathing. Constant doubt. The feeling that life was against me. Concern that I would continue struggling to this degree for the rest of my life.

Is this it? Is this all You have for me, God?

I remember the moment vividly. It was May of 2004 at a campus ministry conference. I was one of the leaders, the teachers, the ones with the knowledge—the answers. Still, I was gasping for air.

Drowning.

Is this it, God?

I was walking around the old campus. There was a castle, and in the castle was a piano. I sat down at the piano to sing, to write, to think. (I sometimes think best while sitting at a piano.) I began to play, and this is what came out:

There must be more than this

Over and over, I sang this to my Lord. Deep down in my soul, I experienced God's fingerprint. I knew He was real. And because I had already seen Him working in so many ways, I had to believe that there was more. I desperately needed to hear His voice tell me that all this striving, all this seeking wasn't for nothing.

This couldn't be all the Christian life had to offer.

There must be more than this

Oh, my God, is this really all there is?

Later that week, as I continued to cry out to God, He spoke clearly to me concerning some of my questions and struggles. Most of all, He called me to choose to trust Him, to rest in Him, and to allow Him to teach me. He beckoned me to go on a journey with Him, a journey to further wholeness and freedom, choosing to believe He is who He says He is.

> Come to me, all you who are weary and burdened, and
> I will give you rest. Take my yoke upon you and learn
> from me, for I am gentle and humble in heart, and you
> will find rest for your souls. For my yoke is easy and my
> burden is light. (Matthew 11:28–30)

Thus began this journey into my current understanding of true freedom. (You can read a full testimony in the back of this book.) I'm sure it's not over. I invite you to join me where I am now.

I imagine that you are reading this book because you are at least interested in the claims of Jesus and the freedom that we Christians say He offers.

Maybe you already believe in Jesus and follow Him. Yet the questions linger. The mundane feels overwhelming. The warm fuzzy feelings have worn off. You wonder if God still cares about your lingering challenges and the patterns of thinking or behavior that plague you.

Maybe your faith still feels as fresh and alive as ever, but you simply seek a deeper level of freedom than you've experienced thus far.

You may not be sure you really know God, or you may be quite confident that you don't. You may not be sure that you want to know Him anymore. Perhaps you have experienced a measure of freedom, have long since moved past that "gasping for air" feeling, but still dream and hope, as I did, for more than this.

This book is for you all.

There are a lot of ways you could use this book. You could read it all in one sitting. You could read it in small chunks and pause to ponder the various Scriptures. I encourage you to grab a Bible, a journal or paper, and a pen. Ask the Holy Spirit to guide your time and open your eyes to what you need to hear. Ask God, the Giver of life, to breathe life into each freedom step. If a Scripture reference is mentioned, look it up in the translation you have, read the context, reflect on that Scripture, and consider writing in your journal. Reflect on each section and ask yourself the study questions in the back of the book. Continually pray as you read and ask God to speak truth and life into your heart.

Wherever you are on this journey, there is something to be learned from Him. Even if you're not generally a praying person, I encourage you to pause. Pray the following for yourself as inspired by the Scripture above and prepare to dive into a new level of freedom in your life:

> *God, I come to You. I am weary, burdened, and I need Your rest. God, I lay down my heavy burden and take Your yoke upon my shoulders, whatever that means, because You say I can learn from You, in Your gentleness and humility of heart. Your yoke is easy and Your burden is light. God, help me to receive that, and prepare me to really hear from You as I read this book. I surrender to all that You have for me as I learn to walk in freedom. Amen.*

INTRODUCTION TO FREEDOM

YEARS AGO, as I clung to Jesus in an effort to understand why I was not experiencing the fullness of His freedom in my life, I began to ask the following questions:

What is freedom?

What does the Bible have to say about freedom?

Is freedom attainable?

If so, what does freedom look like?

Jesus said He came to "proclaim freedom for the prisoners" (Luke 4:18). Galatians 5:1 says, "It is for freedom that Christ has set us free."

In the New Testament, several words are translated as "freedom" or "liberty." They describe a state of being *exempt, free from slavery, free from the dominion of sin, or independent.*[1] True freedom, however, is not just liberation from sin or bondage. The freedom that Jesus died for is also the freedom to discover who God really is, who you are in relation to Him, and the specific person He created you to be. It is the freedom to live in the fullness of all He has for you.

I believe freedom is one of the most misunderstood topics in Christianity.

I certainly didn't understand what it meant or felt like. I looked around the church and saw that my experience and lack of understanding was not unique. Most Christians seem to reside in one of two extremes. The first group, if asked, would agree that God is able to do the impossible. To deny this would be to say Jesus was lying in Luke 1:37 when He said, "Nothing is impossible with God." But one can see by the way they act, think, and live that they don't really believe God wants to do anything extraordinary in their lives or with their struggles.

The other group of believers have an unrealistic idea of what freedom looks like and how the process of learning to walk in freedom should progress. They expect some sort of "zap" experience wherein temptations and struggles disappear in a moment. The Bible says we are a new creation, so shouldn't we be free immediately?

Let me explain what I see as the middle ground between these two beliefs.

I believe Scripture teaches that freedom is both a one-time gift and a process. The moment we come to Jesus Christ, He gives us freedom through the Holy Spirit, so that we are no longer slaves to sin (Romans 6:17–18), but that freedom is something we need to learn to walk out in our lives.

Paul's letters to the New Testament churches often used the analogy of the Christian life being like running a race or training to be an athlete. Elite athletes already have the gifts and natural talents they need to develop into that athlete when they are born, but you would never put a newborn at the starting line of a marathon and expect to see him at the end.

First, he needs to learn to roll over. After a while, a baby generally devises a method of dragging himself across the floor. Eventually, he crawls, and after a while longer, he learns to walk. In taking these first steps, he will stumble and fall. And sometimes succeed. Eventually, he can jog. And then run. And the first run he goes on will probably not set a world record.

He must *train* to become an elite athlete, even though the potential is there.

As believers in and followers of Jesus Christ, it is the same for us. While in that moment when we first come to Christ we have everything we need for life and godliness (2 Peter 1:3) and we are free in Christ (John 8:36, Galatians 5:1,13), we still need to learn to walk out that freedom. We need to train ourselves to respond differently than in the past, both in the way we act and in the way we think. If this freedom were something that came about in a "zap" moment, then the direction offered to believers in the New Testament books of Romans through Jude would be unnecessary.

1 John 3:9 says that we have God's seed in us; the RSV renders this "God's nature abides in him," that is, in the child of God.

If I took a packet of seeds and planted one in the ground today, you would not go outside in an hour and expect to see a plant. The seed needs to be tended to. It needs to be watered, it needs sunlight, it needs certain weather conditions, but mostly it needs time.

John Stott says that "the new birth involves the acquisition of a new nature through the implanting within us of the very seed or lifegiving power of God."[2] At salvation, God gives us all we need to learn to walk in freedom. That seed planted in us must be tended in order to experience the fullness of all He has for us.

We can look at freedom from another angle by considering how we came to lack freedom in the first place.

How did we get here?

As believers, we often say that Jesus came to solve the problem of sin. He came so that we can be in relationship with God and be with God for eternity.

Jesus did in fact come so that we may have eternal life. Most of us know the oft-quoted verse, John 3:16: "For God so loved the world that he gave his one and only Son, that whoever believes in him shall not perish but have eternal life."

There is another equally important reason Jesus came. He states in John 10:10 (NASB): "The thief comes only to steal and kill and destroy; *I came that they may have life, and have it abundantly.*" (emphasis mine)

I believe Jesus was not only talking about eternity here; He was talking about our life here on earth.

We can find another aspect of Jesus' mission by going back to the Garden of Eden. Genesis 1:26–27 describes the creation of mankind:

> Then God said, "Let us make man in our image, in our
> likeness, and let them rule over the fish of the sea and the
> birds of the air, over the livestock, over all the earth, and
> over all the creatures that move along the ground." So
> God created man in his own image, in the image of God
> he created him; male and female he created them.

God created Adam and Eve in His image; His image was within Adam and Eve. As if this weren't amazing enough, we read Genesis 2:7: "The LORD God formed the man from the dust of the ground and breathed into his nostrils the breath of life, and the man became a living being."

God not only gave them life through shaping them, creating them and giving them His image and likeness; He went a step further by breathing His very breath into them.

He was their source of life.

In the Garden, God walked with man. He spent time with man. That all changed when Adam and Eve ate from the tree of the knowledge of good and evil.[3] When they ate from this tree, not only did they pass down sin to generations to come (and thus, our current need for reconciliation with God), they also became disconnected from their source of life.[4]

Remember John 10:10: "The thief comes only to steal and kill and destroy." This is exactly what the serpent did in the Garden. He stole their freedom from sin and the freedom they had to walk in close, intimate relationship with God the Father. He also killed them in the sense that they would now age and die, and he destroyed the connection they had with their source of life.

"I [Jesus] came that they may have life, and have it abundantly" (John 10:10, NASB).

Jesus certainly came to rectify the problem of sin in our lives by becoming the perfect sacrifice for our sins on the cross and by being resurrected —brought back to life. He nullifies the killing, stealing and destroying of Satan by reconciling us to God (2 Corinthians 5:19)—in other words, reconnecting us with the ultimate source of life.

God is the source of life and the giver of freedom through Jesus Christ. The five freedom steps are to be used as guides as we learn to walk in the fullness of the freedom that is available to those who are adopted children of God.

FREEDOM STEP ONE:
Spend Time with the Freedom Giver

FOR THE PAST 10 YEARS, I have worked with Christians dealing with unwanted same-sex attraction. People often come for help because they can't figure out how to be set free from this particular temptation.

There are a few problems with approaching our issues this way.

First, we are never promised a life free of temptation. James 1:13 states, "Let no one say when he is tempted, 'I am being tempted by God'" (NASB). Notice the verse says "when" he is tempted, not "if." Jesus was tempted, but did not sin. If we expect a life free from temptation, then we expect to be more free than Jesus. Temptation is to be expected, but we can learn to practice God-empowered self-control in how we respond.

Second, when we spend our lives micro-managing a particular struggle, we quickly lose sight of the bigger picture. We are not simply the sum of our problems. Our identity should not be defined by our struggles or temptations. Our identity is defined by our Creator, our Heavenly Father.

1 Corinthians 6:9–11 lists a string of offenders who will not inherit the kingdom of God. And then, the punch line: "That is what some of you *were.*" (emphasis mine)

Our identity as believers in Jesus Christ no longer lies in how our struggle with sin manifests itself! We are new creations, adopted children of the Most High God. Our identity now rests in God alone. And all our problems wouldn't go away if this one struggle magically and instantaneously disappeared. Counselor and pastor Bob Hamp said, "Freedom is not the absence of something; it's the presence of someone."[5] Our freedom is found in one place: God, the Freedom Giver.

Let me be very clear. I am not saying: "If you simply spent more time with God, you wouldn't be facing the issues you are now." Lots of people dealing with life-controlling issues, particularly those of a sexual nature, have been told ad nauseam that if they pray and read the Bible more, then they will no longer experience that particular temptation. Yes, Bible reading and prayer are pieces of the puzzle, but they are not the whole picture. However, the reason I encourage you to spend time with the Freedom Giver first is strategic.

> You made all the delicate, inner parts of my body
> and knit me together in my mother's womb.
> Thank you for making me so wonderfully complex!
> Your workmanship is marvelous—how well I know it.
> (Psalm 139:13–14, NLT)

God made you. He made you for more—more than merely struggling through life, gasping for air. More than grasping at whatever you can find to fill the emptiness. More than you can think or imagine.

You were knit together by the hand of God, the Freedom Giver. From the beginning of time, God had a plan in mind to rescue humanity, that His creations might know Him fully through the freedom that Jesus would die to bring. He has called you by name and said, "You are mine. I have made you for more." In God we find who we are and who He created us to be. Remember Adam and Eve. God was their literal source of life. He breathed His very breath into them after shaping them with His own hands. God has done the same to us, not only in His creation of us, but in breathing His Holy Spirit into us as believers.

Thus, we cannot know ourselves without truly knowing our Creator and Father. And yet, we often recoil at the idea of God as Father. We sigh with feelings of inadequacy when told to spend time with Him. Or we simply don't bother to try.

Why is that?

Think of a person you care deeply about or of a time you had just begun a relationship with someone. Would someone have had to drag you, kicking and screaming, to spend time with that person? That just doesn't happen. You think about that person often. You imagine the next time you can get together. And you find ways to connect until you can see each other face to face.

Do you feel that way about God, dreaming of the next opportunity you get to spend concentrated time with Him? What might be keeping you from feeling that way?

God's words, found in Psalm 50:21, say "You thought I was altogether like you."

Stop for a minute and ask yourself the question: who do you think God is? Try not to answer immediately, but ask God to search your heart. If you were raised in church, suppress the answers you learned in Sunday School, from your pastor or from your parents. Try to separate what you know in your head from what you believe in your heart to be true.

Who do you think God is?

Pay attention to what you are experiencing. When you think about God and His character, what kind of feelings rise up within you? Warm and loving feelings? Angry and frustrated feelings? Brokenhearted feelings? Feelings of longing and loneliness?

Deep in your heart, what do you really think about God? What is His nature, His character?

God through His Word gives us the opportunity to learn who He really is. Spending time with Him gives Him the space to reveal Himself to us. In Psalm 139:7–10, we learn there is nowhere we can go and *not* be in God's presence. But while we're always in His presence, that doesn't mean we're actually spending purposeful time cultivating our relationship with Him. To illustrate the difference between being in God's presence and spending time with Him, I'll share an analogy from my life.

I talk to my husband almost every day. Most days, it's just mundane stuff: what's for dinner, what the kids need, what's on the schedule for the coming week. Even though I am in his presence quite frequently, it's not the same as sitting down and spending time with him, as undistracted as possible. If a few days go by without the opportunity to sit down and actually look each other in the eyes for a few minutes, I miss it. Finding this time is increasingly difficult with two small kids, but it's important, so we make it happen.

We can't be in a relationship with someone we don't know. And we cannot surrender our struggles and grow to trust someone we don't know *deeply*.

What does it mean to know the Freedom Giver? How do we grow to know Him more intimately?

Know the Freedom Giver as loving father. As believers, we have been adopted into God's family as His children; no concern or desire is too small for God. This has struck me on an even deeper level since I had my sons.

Though it can be unbelievably challenging to be a mom, there is no joy like having a child. It has helped me to understand God's heart for His children in a whole new way. I get so excited about every little thing my kids do.

"Oh, my goodness! He stuck out his tongue! Wasn't that amazing?"

"Wow! He's getting teeth!"

"He smiled at me and grabbed my hair!"

"Did you hear what he just said? He's so clever!"

Then, we post it all on Facebook, so our friends and family know how amazing our child is. I joke, but isn't that what you see on your Facebook feed?

It's amazing to think that this is how our God rejoices over every little discovery and victory in our lives. Except for the part about posting on Facebook, but can you imagine how busy His feed would be?

I also am amazed at how much I love my kids—so much love for someone who comes into this world completely helpless. Babies don't give us any particularly compelling reason to love them. Yet after my first son was born, I caught myself thinking, *Wow, is this how much my parents love me?* He hasn't done anything to earn or deserve my love; I love him simply because he is my child.

So often we try to earn God's love by our actions. Or we worry that we've lost God's love when we struggle with sin, doubt, or unbelief. God loves us simply because we're His creations, His children. And He loves me (and you!) far more than I could ever love my son. That is unfathomable.

God, the Freedom Giver, is not far off. In fact, He is "close to the brokenhearted and saves those who are crushed in spirit" (Psalm 34:18). "Those who seek the LORD lack no good thing" (Psalm 34:10). He abounds in love to us (Psalm 86:15).

We can see God's fatherly and freedom-giving character all through His Word. The things He desires for His children are good things. The next time you open the Bible, take the time to listen to, and learn about, God's heart. If there's something you don't understand or can't make sense of, ask Him for help and wisdom (James 1:5), which God gives generously. He loves us more than we can fathom and is concerned about our everyday needs in a way that we cannot even imagine, including our need to understand who He is through His Word.

Know the Freedom Giver's true character through His Word. In order to experience true freedom, we must know the Freedom Giver deeply. We must know His character, His heart. We must learn to rest in Him in order to discover who He created us to be and the freedom found there. We must allow His Spirit to invade every part of our lives. And we must dive into the Word of God with a heart open to how God might be found there.

James 1:22 says, "Do not merely listen to the word, and so deceive yourselves. Do what it says."

Part of doing what it says is living like we believe what we read. What would happen if you chose to believe what the Bible has to say about God?

What would happen if you choose to believe that He is good? Faithful? Just? Able to do the impossible? Compassionate? Slow to anger? Patient? What would happen if you chose to believe that the things the Bible says about God's character are true?

Let me ask another question. What would happen if you chose to believe that He cares about all the little details of your daily life? That He loves your desire to see a new level of freedom in your life?

> "Are not two sparrows sold for a penny? Yet not one of them will fall to the ground apart from the will of your Father. And even the very hairs of your head are all numbered. So don't be afraid; you are worth more than many sparrows." (Matthew 10:29–31)

Reading God's Word is a great way to begin to learn about Him, to connect with the source of life and the giver of freedom. We can also learn from Him through practicing the spiritual disciplines. *Here are a few examples.*

Serve. One way to spend time with the Freedom Giver is through service. It can be an amazing tool of growth and learning, even for a young believer. I'm not encouraging people to begin ministries of their own the day after they become Christians. Even the apostle Paul took time, lots of time, before he began to minister. That said, anyone can mop the floor of the church or serve a cup of soup at a homeless shelter.

Serving cultivates gratitude and compassion, as well as perspective. Jesus said that when we serve, it is as if we are serving Him (Matthew 25:40). Through serving, God's heart is revealed for the people He created. It reminds us of His deep love for others, His concerns for their needs, and His promises and plans for their lives. Through seeing those truths in the lives of others, we are reminded that those things are true for us, as well. Serving also points us toward our gifts. As we learn where our strengths and weaknesses lie, we gather insight into who God created us to be. We must beware of becoming like the church in Ephesus (Revelation 2:1–6), who served God with all their hearts, but had lost a passion and a true love for the Person they were serving. They stopped resting in Him and using that place of rest as their source of strength (1 Peter 4:11).

Practice silence and solitude. Another important discipline that can help us get to know the Freedom Giver is silence and solitude. Psalm 46:10 says, "Be still, and know that I am God." The NASB translates it this way: "Cease striving and know that I am God." When we become still, we create the space we need to really know, and thus experience, God.

There are so many things in this world that cry out for our attention, and it can become increasingly difficult to quiet them. We need to still the noise, the clamor, and the chatter of our lives and just wait.

Back at that campus ministry conference I mentioned earlier in this book, I cried out to God to show me more. You may remember that the cry of my heart was, *There must be more than this.* God did speak to me, and what He said surprised me. In the quietness of my heart, I heard Him say that He had a plan for me that would "blow your small ambitions out of the water." Then He told me that I wasn't ready to hear that plan.

That was not what I wanted to hear.

He told me I needed to learn the truth of Psalm 46:10, that in the stillness of resting, not in the busyness of activity, was where I would truly grow to know Him. He showed me that learning to walk in freedom begins with resting: resting in Him, growing to trust Him, learning to run straight to Him with trials, confusion, and pain. I needed to allow Him to fill me with His spirit in order to have anything to offer to anyone else. I needed to make time to just sit and allow Him to heal me.

Jesus knew the discipline of silence and solitude well. He had both short and long periods of silence, solitude, prayer, and fasting. You, too, can find little pockets of solitude in your day. Early in the morning when you first wake up. Washing dishes. Sitting in traffic. Since having kids, sometimes I just sit quietly and take deep breaths as I watch them play. I'm a runner, and I use that time to clear my head and focus on my Lord. I struggle with focusing on prayer if I try to simply sit and pray alone, so I recently began praying while I walk through my neighborhood early in the morning.

Beyond those little moments, we can search out longer periods where we sit or walk in silence and allow God to work in our lives. We may not hear anything specifically. Actually, we can frustrate ourselves (as I did) if we try too hard to hear, but our simple prayer can be that God would work into our hearts the knowledge of who He is and who we are in Him. Our sole desire can be to reconnect with our source of life and giver of freedom.

One of my mentors goes on an annual, 24-hour, silent retreat. This may not be possible for you, but what about an hour?

Sitting silently before God for an hour, possibly meditating on a verse of Scripture that is challenging, might be unfathomable. Start with five minutes. We don't have any trouble meditating on things we are passionate about. If you're a big fan of a particular actor or a sport, for instance, do you have to remind yourself to go see the latest movie or to watch the play-offs? Do you have to put it on your to-do list? No, of course not! In fact, the thought of seeing these things likely consumes much of your thoughts in the days beforehand.

How do we grow to be that passionate about God and knowing Him deeply? We make the time and space to rest in God's presence, to not only learn to trust Him, but also to surrender to Him those areas of our lives that we've attempted to keep from Him. We allow Him to know us deeply, too (Matthew 7:22–23).

When was the last time you carved out a span of time to sit quietly before God? Have you ever done this? Does the very thought of it frighten you?

If you have tried to do this, think back on a recent occasion, possibly even when I asked you to consider who you think God is earlier in this Freedom Step.

What rose up in you when you tried to sit quietly before God?

My early times of silence and solitude were very telling, as I realized how much of my relational experiences with others and my view of myself was being projected onto God (Psalm 50:21 again). These times also showed me the truth of what I believed about God, His character, and His concern for me, as some of my false core beliefs about God rose to the surface.

Core beliefs is a concept I learned from pastor and counselor Russell Willingham. To explain it briefly here (it will be explained more thoroughly below), we all have stated beliefs and core beliefs. While stated beliefs are those things we say are true, our behavior, emotions and lifestyle flow directly from core beliefs.

During my early times of silence and solitude, if God didn't show up in specific ways, my heart assumed He was cold, heartless, uninterested in my effort to connect with Him, distant, hard to get to know, and unloving. Of course, my stated belief was that God was loving, kind, compassionate, and close to the brokenhearted, but in those times of silence, it became clear to me that my core beliefs were something quite different.

Or, I thought, maybe the problem was *me*. Maybe God was kind and loving toward others, but I was so flawed that He could not love me unconditionally. (This is addressed more extensively in Freedom Steps Four and Five.)

Part of the issue was that I was approaching God to get. There is nothing wrong with going to God with a specific need or with a hope that you will receive something from Him. God is a good father who doesn't give His kids stones when they ask for bread (Matthew 7:9). However, when I approached God with my need, I had a strong idea of what I wanted to get out of the experience. When the time didn't go according to my plan, it then confirmed all the false core beliefs that I held, some of which I stated above.

Rather than approaching God with an agenda, we can use these silent times to connect with Him, simply to come into His presence as we are with no expectations other than to love Him and be loved by Him. When we do have a need or a desire, we choose to surrender that need to our loving Father, believing that ultimately, His best will happen in our lives.

Let me more fully explain "core beliefs." I have found this concept to be foundational not only in connecting with the Freedom Giver, but in the overall process of learning to walk in freedom.

We all have stated beliefs. We all have core beliefs. Here's a way to illustrate the difference.

Imagine I hang a weight from the ceiling with a string. I have you stand back from that weight so that when I draw the weight back, it is level with your head.

Before dropping the weight, thus letting it swing like a pendulum, I remind you of the laws of pendulum motion, in particular, that when the weight swings back toward you, it will stop before touching you. I ask you if you believe the laws of physics. You say yes. I drop the weight, and when it swings back toward your head, you jump out of the way.

Your stated belief in the laws of physics was insufficient to overcome your core belief that something heavy hurtling at your head will cause harm.[6]

Core beliefs are those beliefs we have deep inside our hearts that are the guiding principles of our lives, states Russell Willingham. They often contradict what we claim to believe as Christians. We say we believe one thing (stated belief), but our actions, feelings, and choices demonstrate that we believe something else (core belief).[7]

Here is one example. Most Christians would say they trust God, explicitly and unconditionally. Yet when faced with a trial, our true core belief, that God is not trustworthy, drives our actions. Sometimes, we do pray, but then we continue to live in constant fear and anxiety, imagining and dreading all the possible outcomes to the trial. That said, rarely is our first instinct to go to prayer. First we worry, and then we think fretfully about whether or not God will move in this situation. We decide God never shows up when we need Him to, so we had better do something, since He certainly isn't going to.

If our core belief is that God really can be trusted, we would pray and leave our trial with God. When worry starts to rise to the surface (and a worrying thought does not necessarily equate to distrust of God), we once again pray and turn that worry over to God. And do that again. And again. Trusting God doesn't necessarily mean we don't do anything to rectify the situation, but rather we trust in God as our source to guide and direct us in the midst of the trial.

If your behavior contradicts your Christianity, if your feelings and your actions don't match what you say you believe as a Christian, then your core beliefs are different from your stated beliefs.

When I would sit quietly before God, what I really believed to be true about God would rise to the surface. My core beliefs, those beliefs that my actions and feelings flowed out of, were so clearly different than my stated beliefs. When I faced a crisis or a situation that felt overwhelming, my heart jumped to the false core belief that God didn't really care about my needs or my worries. I needed God to renew my heart, to reveal Himself to me as a good Father. I also needed to choose to trust that He is who He says He is and He will do what He has said He will do (I will share more fully about how God transformed my mind in Freedom Step Four).

Psalm 119:45 says, "I will walk about in freedom, for I have sought out your precepts." I needed to learn who the Bible says God is in order to attack those false core beliefs, as knowing God, His Word and His principles brings freedom. "Quiet times" or "devotionals" (as we often call the times we set aside to spend with God) don't have to look like sitting in a chair and reading the Bible. Use a devotional book if that works best for you. It could mean taking a prayer hike and listening to the Bible on your iPod, or blasting worship tunes and dancing in your living room. It could mean going to a nursing home and doing a Bible study with some of the residents. Feel free to be creative. Gary Thomas' book, *Sacred Pathways*, has some great suggestions.[8] Practice a lifestyle of hearing, listening, and waiting on God while choosing to trust in Him to meet your needs.

I'm at the point in my life where I notice a big difference in myself, my thoughts, my actions, and my words when I don't spend time with God, praying, resting, hearing, waiting, and reading His Word. This wasn't always the case. There have been plenty of times in my life that I did these things simply because I knew it was the right thing to do and would be beneficial. Eventually, I was able to see the difference those things made in my daily life.

Ask God to build in you a desire to seek Him, but don't wait for that desire to appear. Do it with a belief that God will show up if you show up.

"Draw near to God and He will draw near to you" (James 4:8a, NASB).

Free people spend time with the Freedom Giver: Freedom Step One.

FREEDOM STEP TWO:
Spend Time with Freedom Seekers

And let us consider how we may spur one another on toward love and good deeds. Let us not give up meeting together, as some are in the habit of doing, but let us encourage one another—and all the more as we see the Day approaching. (Hebrews 10:24–25)

IN WESTERN SOCIETY, we are raised to be self-reliant. Many of us have been taught from a young age that self-sufficiency and independence are qualities to be admired and obtained. We praise infants who sleep through the night, starting sleep training at 4–6 months. We applaud young children who learn to play alone for long periods of time, but when they get to school we grade them on whether they play well with others.

An anthropologist who studied child-rearing in middle class America in comparison to tropical Africa wrote:

> A pervasive theme of American child-rearing ideology is independence, which can be considered under 3 headings: separateness, self-sufficiency, and self-confidence. The emphasis on separateness begins at birth among middle-class Americans, with the allocation of a separate room to the neonate, requiring him to sleep in his own bed removed from others in the family. American infants experience a particularly sharp distinction between situations where they are alone and those in which they are with others.
>
> American parents begin to emphasize sharing only after the child has become habituated to eating, sleeping, and

being comforted alone, on his own terms, and with his
own properties—which he has become reluctant to give
up.[9]

Rooted in this self-sufficiency syndrome is one of the biggest lies the
enemy of our souls tries to convince us of: All I need in order to learn to
walk in freedom is God and me—no one and nothing else. It sounds true,
because it's so similar to many of the core values of our society. The enemy
of our souls runs with those values and tells us that we can figure this out
on our own. The underlying message of this lie turned core belief is that
we will be rejected if we are honest, that we will be abandoned, and that
the shame we feel is because our behavior is uniquely ugly and shameful.

Let me pause a moment and say that I understand the desire to figure
this out on our own. We *are* ashamed. We feel ridiculous, that we should
be able to get over this already. We just don't want to have to tell anyone we
have messed up—again.

While Satan may be the origin of this lie, many of us don't even really
need Satan's help to heap shame on our heads. *What is wrong with me?*
we say to ourselves. *Why can't I figure out how to be self-controlled? Why
do I keep repenting, promising God I'll never do it again, only to find myself
repenting again of the same thing in a day, week, month, or year?*

Have you experienced this?

Even prior to becoming a believer, I prayed that God would somehow
miraculously change me by taking away my eating disorder (as long as I
didn't have to get fat!) and making me straight. I prayed earnestly, and God
did not take these things away. I used this as evidence that God created me
to be a lesbian, thus embracing my gay identity and getting on with my life.

I find this experience of shame to be quite common, especially among
those raised in church. They didn't see demonstrations of healthy vulnerability and honest struggling in their role models. When they realize they
are struggling with something of which they feel deeply ashamed (whatever that might be), they take that thing to God and plead, as Paul described
in 2 Corinthians 12:8, for God to remove it from them. When He doesn't
respond in the way they were hoping, many in the church come to believe
that God is either unwilling or unable to help. Tragically, too few consider
that God might have designed a way to find freedom other than prayer in
isolation.

Shame causes us to embrace the false core belief, *If I am honest, I will be abandoned.*[10] It is shame that keeps us from going to church because we've had a bad week and don't want to have to tell anyone about it. It is shame that makes us choose to stay home from a fellowship event when we are fighting with our spouse. It is shame that tells us to put on a smiley face and say everything is great when we feel as if we are dying inside.

But Jesus died on the cross so that you could be set free from that shame.

Hopefully, you are reading this book because you desperately want to believe that freedom is possible, healing still happens, and Jesus died for something more than what you have experienced thus far in your struggles.

Jesus spent a lot of time telling the disciples how to act with unbelievers, but He spent even more time telling us how to treat fellow believers and what we can learn from each other. The authors of the New Testament letters also discussed our relationship as believers at length.

There are at least forty-six occurrences of *one another* and *each other* directives in the New Testament. The most common one is the command to love one another. The Bible instructs believers repeatedly not only to love one another, but to admonish, to submit to, to instruct, to encourage, and to offer hospitality to each other. How do we learn how to do this? In the company of other freedom seekers!

In Acts 2, we can see how purposeful the early Christians were about living in close community. Verse 44 says, "All the believers were together and had everything in common." What a thought-provoking picture of how to teach one another to be disciples, to encourage each other, and to "spur one another on," as the author of Hebrews writes.

Jesus' words in the passage below highlight how important it is that once people hear the Gospel and believe it, we teach those people the principles and concepts that Jesus has taught us.

> Go therefore and make disciples of all the nations,
> baptizing them in the name of the Father and of the Son
> and of the Holy Spirit, teaching them to observe all that
> I commanded you; and lo, I am with you always, even to
> the end of the age. (Matthew 28:19–20, NASB)

One such concept is how to walk in freedom. Freedom is part of being a disciple. And learning to heal and learning to walk out our freedom always happen in the context of community. These aren't things we can learn alone.

James 5:16 says, "Confess your sins to one another, and pray for one another so that you may be healed" (NASB). Notice it doesn't say, "Confess your sins to God alone." As believers, we cannot experience freedom without the willingness to look at ourselves and to allow others to look at us with brutal honesty.

There is something about confessing our sins and allowing others to speak into our lives that breaks the power of the secrecy and shame of our sin. It lets light in, and when we live in the light, the darkness must flee (1 John 1:5). Bringing our struggles into the light can silence the lies we're believing about ourselves, about our sin and even about God. Ultimately, it brings healing and freedom into our lives.

There have been many times when being in relationship with others has helped me to learn to walk in freedom. I think of my first Bible study leader, Melissa. The first time we met for lunch, I told her everything about me—my struggles with same-sex attraction, self-injury, disordered eating, and so on. I fully expected her to be disgusted and run out of the restaurant! But she did exactly the opposite. She lovingly welcomed me not only to Bible study, but also into her life. Through her, I learned that I could truly love a woman, be in close friendship with her, and not be tempted to be in a sexual relationship with her.

I think of my therapist of three years, Elizabeth. She continually reminded me of who I was in Christ and gently challenged my faulty ways of thinking (I talk about this more in Freedom Step Four).

My friend Judy taught me how to really experience the depth of grace. (I'll mention her again in Freedom Step Three.)

In John 11, Jesus raised Lazarus from the dead. When Lazarus emerged from the tomb, he still had his grave clothes on him. Why do you think that is? Certainly the God who can supernaturally raise from the dead could also supernaturally free a man from the evidence of death, but Jesus chose not to do so. Instead, Jesus insisted that the crowd be involved in some small way in the healing process. Jesus told those who were there, "Take off the grave clothes and let him go." Who was at the tomb? Mary, Martha and a whole crowd of other people.[11]

Was it an easy suggestion for those people to even consider unwrapping Lazarus? Jews were forbidden to touch a dead person, but, in Lazarus, Jesus saw something quite different.

He saw through the grave clothes. He saw the potential underneath the visible lingerings of death. Jesus saw someone who was once dead, but was now alive. He saw a new creation, and He didn't ask that others be involved in the healing process. He didn't say, "Would you mind taking off his grave clothes?" He commanded that they be involved.

Lazarus could no more have removed his own grave clothes than he could have resurrected himself. Though alive, the evidence of death was all over him. Lazarus needed the help of others to become the free person that he had the potential to be now that Jesus had restored his life.

What a powerful picture for us today! Whether or not Jesus intended to provide His audience with an illustration of the power of being in community, the analogy is compelling. The evidence of death, spiritual death, still lingers in all of us after we become believers in Jesus Christ. Sometimes it is painfully obvious and downright ugly. Other times, it stays insidiously hidden until something triggers it to rise to the surface. Either way, we need other freedom seekers to come alongside us and help free us from the lingering effects spiritual death has in our lives.

In 2 Corinthians 12, mentioned before, Paul shares his experience learning about this very concept when God said to him, "My grace is sufficient for you, for my power is made perfect in weakness" (v. 9). God calls us to utilize His strength, not our own. He never told us to figure out life and struggles alone. That's the farthest from what He wants us to do. Paul says that because of this response, he will boast

> All the more gladly about my weaknesses, so that Christ's power may rest on me. That is why, for Christ's sake, I delight in weaknesses, in insults, in hardships, in persecutions, in difficulties. For when I am weak, then I am strong. (v.9–10)

Paul boasted about his weaknesses to the whole Corinthian church and now to us. Whom do you have in your life who cares enough about you and your growth to listen to you boast the way Paul did? Do you need to develop some safe relationships where you too can boast about your weaknesses?

Which of the two following paragraphs best describes your relationships?

Your relationships are life-giving; they breathe life into you. You walk away from interactions refreshed and encouraged. Your friends are a support to you in becoming who God created you to be: an authentic support, with no hidden agenda. Your friends share your desire for freedom and encourage you to pursue and cultivate other friendships.

OR

Your relationships are life-sucking; you walk away from most encounters feeling exhausted and discouraged. Your friends are jealous of your interactions with others. You sometimes suffocate others with your constant neediness or you find yourself drowning in the needs of someone else.

You might find yourself somewhere between the options I describe. I give those descriptions to highlight our need to develop healthy, healing relationships. As human beings, we are relational. It is the core of our being since Adam walked in the Garden of Eden with God and Eve. Yet we tend to struggle with right relating. We either pretend we don't need anyone, maintain only surface relationships, or become too dependent on one person or one relationship.

You may ask: How do I make new friends? How do I cultivate healthy friendships? Here are some thoughts to ponder.

Remember first that no one is "normal." I've heard it said that normal is a setting on a dryer—it shouldn't be used as a measure for human beings. We all have something we'd rather not share. Look at the Bible and find someone who qualifies as "normal" by today's rather arbitrary standards. You'll be looking for a while!

Make relationships top priority. Decide you will spend time with other people who desire freedom as much as, or even more, than you do. If you are in a healthily functioning, recovery-based support group, that's a great start! Obviously, I believe in them as I've worked with one for years and been part of a few myself as a participant. There is a certain level of honesty and vulnerability generally found in these support groups that you may not experience elsewhere.

In the support group that I led, we had a strong suggestion, in addition to regular church involvement, that people also be involved in a church small group that is not recovery-based. We found this to be an invaluable component of the healing process. Recovery-oriented groups do not provide an accurate representation of what it looks like to build relationships in the broader body of Christ. In church small groups, trust is slowly built, and deeper issues are gradually shared with others. We learn how to open our hearts and lives to others gradually, rather than either wearing our issues on our sleeves or continually hiding our true struggles for fear of being misunderstood or rejected.

Live a life of margin.[12] Just as a piece of paper becomes almost unreadable if it has no margins or paragraph breaks, life becomes unmanageable and unlivable when there is no time for people and healing. It shouldn't take you three months to schedule a coffee date with someone because your days are so full already. Friendships take time to develop and grow, and we need to ensure we have the time to do that. We also cannot be true friends unless we have space built into our schedules to respond to the needs of others, when healthy and appropriate.

Pray. Pray that God would help you establish friendships. Pray that He would bring people into your life who are helpful to you, and to whom you can be helpful.

We need people. Think of Jesus. In a mystery we can't completely understand, He was fully God and fully man, with all the power and knowledge of God, and with all the needs and temptations that we have. Yet there were times when He specifically requested that three disciples (Peter, James, and John) accompany Him somewhere, pray with Him, or just be with Him. If He needed people, then I certainly need people.

If you're still hesitant to open up or don't know what level of honesty is appropriate, consider the level of openness with which Jesus conducted His life. He had His group of acquaintances, the large group of disciples. Within that large group were "the Twelve," as they are referred to in John 6, His good friends. Within the Twelve were Peter, James, and John, His intimate friends. There was a level of transparency He reserved only for those three people. With them, He shared His deepest joys and sorrows. Peter, James, and John were the three disciples with Jesus at His transfiguration (Matthew 17). Jesus sent the other disciples away, except Peter, James, and John, at the house of Jairus, whose daughter He raised from the dead (Luke 8). Then, in the Garden of Gethsemane, Jesus took Peter, James, and John further into the garden with Him in one of His deepest times of need (Mark 14).

We see from these examples that Jesus reserved certain times of His life for a chosen few. We also see that Jesus did not have one single best friend; He had three. In their book *Boundaries*, Henry Cloud and John Townsend write, "We all need more than God and a best friend. We need a group of supportive relationships. The reason is simple: having more than one person in our lives allows our friends to be human. To be busy. To be unavailable at times. To hurt and have problems of their own. To have time alone."[13]

We need a circle of friendships with differing levels of intimacy. Not everyone needs to know all our business, but we need a few people to know most of it. Find people who are not afraid to be weak, who talk about sin and struggle in an honest and redemptive way, people who are givers of grace and not condemnation, but who are also not afraid to speak the truth with love and humility. Please see the resources section at the end for more suggestions of how to do this.

Free people spend time with other freedom seekers: Freedom Step Two.

FREEDOM STEP THREE:
Embrace Grace

THE CONCEPT OF GRACE is something I began to grapple with about five and a half years into my Christian walk. It has become one of the keys in helping me overcome my struggle with habitual sin and self-hatred.

I had a long history, even before I was a Christian, of trying to overcome my struggles using sheer will power. It worked—sometimes. I did have some success overcoming the external ways my issues manifested themselves. Five years after becoming a Christian, I was no longer struggling with an eating disorder, something that had plagued me for thirteen years. I wasn't struggling with same-sex attraction. I wasn't smoking, drinking, cussing, sleeping around, or running with those who do. In my good moments, I felt in many ways that I had arrived.

My success as a Christian, in my own eyes, was based on how I behaved.

However, if I was honest with myself, I still had very, very dark times: moments when a small trigger of some sort—a scowling glance or a thoughtless word from a loved one, a fall or even a simple mistake—would send me spiraling into a place of deep despair and self-loathing.

What is wrong with you, I'd say to myself. *You really messed everything up—AGAIN! You can't seem to get anything right.*

The struggle that this graceless way of life produced became so intense that my friend Judy gently encouraged me to explore grace. She began sending me emails about grace, as well as mailing books and teaching tapes (Yes, people still listened to tapes back then!) on the topic. I slowly realized that while I believed in my heart that I was saved by grace alone, I was demonstrating a different set of core beliefs through my actions.

One such belief was that through rules and my own effort, I could overcome all my struggles. I made up all sorts of rules for myself (and others) in an attempt to measure my faith (and theirs). I believed it would be easier to follow rules than to live in the reality of grace. I don't even think I was aware that grace was available to me in my day-to-day life.

Shortly after Judy encouraged me to explore grace, I heard a pastor preach a sermon on the topic at a conference I was attending.

Honestly, as I sat there listening to him teach, I didn't believe what he was saying. He was quoting the Bible and using the verses in context. It seemed to line up with what I knew about God, His character, and what His Word says about grace, but it was shattering the little box in which I had been living.

Grace simply sounded too good to be true.

At that conference, the pastor informed me and everyone listening that Jesus didn't die just to modify my behavior. *Really? Are you sure,* I thought, because I still had a lot of behaviors I wanted to modify! That's why I had constructed a nice set of rules to encourage my own behavior modification. I also saw a lot of behaviors in others that I thought needed to be modified. (Yes, I was a bit of a Pharisee.) I was demonstrating the core belief that my faith—and the faith of others—should be measured solely by the external changes we had made.

As I wrestled with the teaching I heard, I began to ask the following questions:

> *How exactly does grace help us overcome the cycle of sin?*
>
> *What does God want us to do when we struggle?*

What I had been doing clearly wasn't working. After a mistake, I would walk around like a dog with its tail between its legs. Or I would beat myself up for an amount of time in direct proportion to the seriousness of my sin or mistake. It wasn't always sin I was beating myself up for; I often punished myself for being human. Then I would try by the sheer power of my will to do better and behave appropriately, as defined by my rather arbitrary standards.

God is very clear in how He expects us to react when we struggle:

> Let us therefore come boldly to the throne of grace, that
> we may obtain mercy and find grace to help in time of
> need. (Hebrews 4:16, NKJV)

Another core belief of mine seemed to be this: I can change myself by berating myself. Thus, when I made a mistake, my response was often to resort to name-calling and self-degradation.

All these core beliefs were failing me miserably. Clearly, I needed some new ones! I had constructed these rules and regulations because grace really *is* too good to be true. Maybe that's why we try to accomplish right behavior through rules and our own effort.

Paul knew this would be the tendency of some of us. He saw it in the early church and wrote to the Galatians in chapter 3:

> You foolish Galatians! Who has bewitched you? Before your very eyes Jesus Christ was clearly portrayed as crucified. I would like to learn just one thing from you: Did you receive the Spirit by observing the law, or by believing what you heard? Are you so foolish? *After beginning with the Spirit, are you now trying to attain your goal by human effort?* (v.1–3, emphasis mine)

Trying to be free through rules and human effort injects you into a cycle where *you* are responsible for your own healing. I've found that living this way only heaps shame and condemnation on my head and in the end has no power to make me behave better.

I do believe all this effort was coming from the right place in my heart. I knew that God had been willing to lay down His life so that I could live in abundance. I knew that God loved me and the rest of the world so deeply and passionately that He was willing to sacrifice His only Son so that I could come into relationship with Him. I thought He thus deserved a life laid down, which to me meant good behavior on my part. And how did I try to achieve this good behavior? Not by the power of His Spirit, but by the power of Brenna and Brenna's rules for good, Christian living.

Paul also addressed this problem with the Colossian church:

> Since you died with Christ to the elemental spiritual forces of this world, why, as though you still belonged to the world, do you submit to its rules: "Do not handle! Do not taste! Do not touch!"? These rules, which have to do with things that are all destined to perish with use, are based on merely human commands and teachings. Such

> regulations indeed have an appearance of wisdom, with
> their self-imposed worship, their false humility and their
> harsh treatment of the body, but they lack any value in
> restraining sensual indulgence. (Colossians 2:20–23)

Here's the bottom line: I *cannot* do this myself. All my striving, self-flagellation, penance, and self-condemnation, all my self-imposed rules got me nowhere in my efforts to reform my behavior. As Paul writes to the Colossians, rules have no power to restrain. Human effort will fail us. Trying harder is not the key to overcoming our struggles.

I didn't make any progress in my life by hating myself, but I finally began to grow when I learned to love myself as God loves me. I needed to choose to walk in His grace when I failed. I needed to learn to accept God's love when I made a mistake. I needed to allow God to transform my mind, as Paul writes in Romans 12:2, and renew my thoughts to line up with what the Word of God says about me. (I'll talk about this in Freedom Step Four.) I needed to choose to believe what He says about me.

The only thing that has the power to restrain us from sin is truly knowing, understanding, and experiencing the fullness of His love and grace. We make different choices in our actions and in our thoughts, because He declared and proclaimed us worth knowing, worth loving, and worth creating when He hung from that cross. We make different choices, because God has so much more for us than sin could ever offer. God wants us to know and believe that He is Jehovah Jireh, the God who provides, and He really can meet our needs. Through His grace, we can learn to experience freedom from our life-controlling issues. When we falter, His grace is enough.

Grace requires practice. It requires patience. It's an everyday choice to rest in Him and allow Him to empower you.

So what do we mean by grace? The Greek word that is often translated as *grace* is *charis*. It's used 148 times in the New Testament. Here are a few examples. The English word that *charis* is translated into is in bold. (These four passages are from the NASB.)

In Luke:

> The angel said to her, "Do not be afraid, Mary; for you
> have found **favor** with God." (1:30)

The Child continued to grow and become strong, increasing in wisdom; and the **grace** of God was upon Him. (2:40)

And Jesus kept increasing in wisdom and stature, and in **favor** with God and men. (2:52)

In John 1:14, 16–17:

And the Word became flesh, and dwelt among us, and we saw His glory, glory as of the only begotten from the Father, full of **grace** and truth.... For of His fullness we have all received, and **grace** upon **grace**. For the Law was given through Moses; **grace** and truth were realized through Jesus Christ.

There are many more examples in the book of Acts. Many of the epistles begin and end with the author writing "grace" to the readers, as in Romans, 1 Corinthians, and 2 Corinthians.

In the above passages, Luke and John wrote about how God's grace was all over Jesus. Jesus never sinned and didn't need to experience salvation through God's grace in the way we do, so they must have meant something a little different.

These Scriptures further illustrate that point:

But to each one of us **grace** was given according to the measure of Christ's gift. (Ephesians 4:7, NASB)

You therefore, my son, be strong in the **grace** that is in Christ Jesus. (2 Timothy 2:1, NASB)

These passages imply that receiving grace is not a one-time event, but an ongoing need, as I have slowly learned and at times reluctantly embraced. Grace is a supernatural empowerment that enables us to continue to follow Jesus, to be transformed into His image, and to daily turn our lives over to Him.

Acts 6:8 states, "Now Stephen, a man full of God's grace and power, did great wonders and miraculous signs among the people." Grace and power went hand-in-hand, enabling Stephen to carry out God's supernatural works. Acts 7:46 describes the favor (*charis*) David found in God, and Luke writes about the favor (*charis*) Mary had. Ephesians 4:7 explains that the supernatural gifts and callings are given through grace as Christ apportions it. James 4:6-7 says God gives grace to the humble and that grace enables us to submit to God and resist the devil.

We also have the example of Paul when he shared in 2 Corinthians 12 about the thorn in his flesh. When he asked God three times to take it away, God responded, "My grace is sufficient for you, for power is perfected in weakness." (v.9, NASB) Paul goes on to say, "most gladly, therefore, I will rather boast about my weaknesses, so that the power of Christ may dwell in me." God's all-sufficient grace came to Paul in the form of power to continue His walk with God, even with the thorn in his flesh, whatever that thorn was.

Many more passages demonstrate the depth of the word *charis* and the broadness of all that God means when He speaks this word to us. Beyond the forgiveness of sins, grace offers supernatural power and favor for everyday life and for resisting sin, as well as power for knowing God more fully and for doing God's work. Grace is a state of being, a way of living life and looking at your circumstances that is meant to govern you, drive you, and change you. Grace enables you to be the unique person God created you to be.

I encourage you to go to the Word and pray that God would show you how to live in *charis*, reveal to you His *charis* in your life, fill you with this power to live how He wants you to live, and refresh you with His supernatural power and favor.

We need to embrace grace, in all its fullness of meaning, if we are to walk in freedom. Free people embrace grace: Freedom Step Three.

FREEDOM STEP FOUR:
Think like a Free Person

PROVERBS 23:7 SAYS, "For as he thinks within himself, so he is" (NASB).

When I first became a follower of Jesus, my mind was a very dark place. I knew Jesus loved me deeply and dearly. I was in awe of His sacrifice on the cross. I believed that what His Word said about believers was true, and that meant it was true about me.

Yet my feelings spoke another reality to me.

In those early days, I talked to everyone about Jesus. I dug deep into His Word and spent time with His children. I experienced loads of joy just knowing He had given me new life, a second chance.

Then something would change. A look, a careless word, a fear, a doubt, a reminder of the past: that small trigger would send my thought life spiraling.

> *You are so stupid. Why did you bother to hope that life could be different? Nothing will ever change. You will never really be happy.*

I had a sense deep in my soul that I was worthless, that hope was useless, and that being honest would end in rejection, so I was sure these things were true. The knowledge I had of God, His love, and His grace had not replaced those messages that played in my head on auto-repeat much of the time.

I was taught at some point in my life to trust my feelings. I remember trying to make sense of my sexuality as a teenager and reading in a book that if you have homosexual feelings, if you are attracted to someone of the same gender, then you are gay. Based on my feelings, this book said, I was gay. This became a pattern for me. I relied on my feelings as my understanding of "truth." If I felt something, it was "true." If I didn't feel it, it wasn't "true." Because I allowed the messages (rightfully, they should be called "lies") I had received in my life to inform my current reality, my thoughts and my feelings dictated my truth.

You can imagine that this is a very dangerous way to live. If a situation felt hopeless, then it was certainly hopeless. If I felt like eating something, even when I was no longer hungry, then I should eat it, because after all, I spent years depriving myself of good food through borderline anorexia. If I had strong feelings toward someone, even after becoming a Christian, then I should act on them. I struggled with self-injury since my teenage years, and I once carved a "W" into my leg with a razor blade to stand for "worthless": that's how sure I was that it was true.

At the beginning of this chapter, I quoted Proverbs 23:7: "For as he thinks within himself, so he is." There is a footnote in the NASB, stating that the verse literally means, "For as he reckons in his soul, so he is." I had so many things I had reckoned in my soul. I had not done this consciously. But at various points in my life, I had looked around at how I perceived things were going, and decided that my life experiences simply confirmed the messages I already believed in my heart. *It's not safe to be yourself. No one likes you as you are. If you are honest, you will probably be rejected.*

As a Christian, I became convicted that if my thoughts were leading me to sin or to clearly harm myself, then I should stop listening to those thoughts, yet the internal battle continued. My thoughts about myself and about God were still filled with those old messages. Those messages not only kept me bound to false ideas about my identity and about God, they kept me from progressing and growing into the child of God He created me to be.

I needed to learn to think like a free person.

I'm still amazed at how God orchestrated what followed. I was two and a half years into knowing Jesus, but I was still struggling heavily with an eating disorder. I was about a year into knowing Roy, a young man I was dating, and realized that if we ever actually got married, I would make a horrible wife if I were still starving myself half the time. On a friend's recommendation, I sought the help of a Christian counselor to overcome my eating disorder.

I remember sitting with my counselor one day, sharing one of these old messages that seemed so true to me, and hearing her say, "That's not what Jesus says about you!" with a big smile on her face. I still tear up just thinking about that moment. I remember wondering, *It's not? What does Jesus say about me?*

This was the beginning of my journey toward thinking like a free person.

Romans 12:2 (NLT) says, "Let God transform you into a new person by changing the way you think." I didn't realize when I walked into that counselor's office that one of the keys to ending my struggle with food and other self-destructive patterns was to literally change the way I thought. I hadn't recognized that much of what I *did* was tied up in what I *thought*. Thus, I could not address my behavior without addressing my ways of thinking; the two could not be separated.

I needed my entire thought life to be transformed, not just in the *things* I was thinking, but the *way* my mind worked. My patterns of thinking—the fear of abandonment, my feelings of worthlessness, the distrust I had toward men, the emotional dependency toward women—were so deeply ingrained that I could not identify those patterns by myself, nor could I recognize how much they contributed to my struggles. It wasn't simply that I had moments of feeling worthless and unlovable; in the core of my being, I was sure it was true. I share more about this in my testimony at the end of this book.

Thinking like a free person took me years to learn. In fact, I'm still working on it. My mind seemed to be filled with contradicting opinions: a combination of what God was teaching me, the things I was taught growing up, and the lies I believed about myself. It was all jumbled together and I could not determine which message was coming from whom. Much of the time, I assumed my thoughts were speaking truth to me (whether they were positive or negative), *because they confirmed how I felt.* They were the only truth I knew, because of the experiences that had skewed my perspective. I could not discern the source of my thoughts, and I did not question the truth of many of the lies I believed.

All believers experience this on some level. Even with the Holy Spirit guiding us and directing us, we still find ourselves needing to fight against our old ways of thinking, ways that are often quite deeply ingrained in us.

Think about some of the thoughts you've had in the recent past. Were they encouraging and life-giving? Or were they soul-crushing?

Many of my ways of thinking sprang out of the false core beliefs I held. These core beliefs were sometimes based on messages I had received from a young age, and sometimes, they were simply based on how I perceived things. As I began to learn to think like a free person, I needed to recognize where the lies and false core beliefs had come from.

Satan is the father of lies. Lies are his native language (John 8:44). The lies we've chosen to believe, that we've allowed to sink in and take root in us, whether they were spoken by our parents, someone we love, or even spoken by ourselves to ourselves, really originated from Satan, the enemy of our souls. We've bought into so many lies about who we are and who God is, and we need to declare war on those lies. We need to trust in God's truth. We literally need to take up that truth: the truth of who God says we are and who He says He is. We need to invite God to breathe life into that truth and use it against the lies of the enemy.

It's a battle to undo the effects of these lies we've believed for years. 2 Corinthians 10:4 says, "The weapons we fight with are not the weapons of the world. On the contrary, they have divine power to demolish strongholds." What comes to mind when you consider the word "strongholds"? If you've pondered this term before, you may think of only the really big stuff like addictions or compulsions. But isn't anything that keeps us from knowing God fully a "stronghold"? Aren't these lies and false core beliefs strongholds? They keep us from knowing God and believing the truth He speaks about us.

In Christ, we have the power to tear down strongholds. Read the following verse, 2 Corinthians 10:5:

> We demolish arguments and every pretension that sets
> itself up against the knowledge of God, and we take
> captive every thought to make it obedient to Christ.

The NASB uses "speculations" instead of arguments. We spend years trying to make sense of what we are experiencing, and these "speculations" are often in direct opposition to what God's Word has to say about our struggles and, more importantly, about us.

These verses make it clear that this battle mainly takes place in our minds. We are commanded to take captive every thought and make it obedient to Christ. Our thoughts should agree with what God says about us and how He views us. Anything that doesn't meet that strict criterion needs to be demolished.

Think of a thought pattern that has been prevalent in your life lately. Maybe you are facing a challenging situation and you are struggling to believe that God is going to provide for you. Maybe your thoughts look something like this:

> *I can't see how God is going to provide for me in this situation, at least not in a timely manner. I feel as if I always have to do everything myself. He could make this easier, and He isn't!*

Sound familiar? What do you think would happen if you counteracted those false beliefs with God's Word?

> *Wow, God, this is a really tough situation I'm in. But I know that You will meet all my needs according to the riches of Your glory in Christ Jesus (Philippians 4:19). I also know that the lions may grow weak and hungry, but those who seek the LORD lack no good thing (Psalm 34:10). I am worth more than many small birds (Luke 12:7), and You are a good father who doesn't give His kids stones when they ask for bread (Matthew 7:9). Lord, I believe; help change my thoughts and the areas where I struggle with unbelief (Mark 9:24). Make these truths come alive by breathing life into them through Your Holy Spirit.*

I remember some very painful and tear-filled prayer times in my early walk with God. I'd cry out to God, "I can't feel you, God! Please be here with me." Satan tried to use that against me. "See, you can't feel God! He doesn't like you anymore! Na-na-nuh-boo-boo!" Of course if he had actually said, "Na-na-nuh-boo-boo!" maybe I would have seen clearly where these thoughts came from.

I realized that thinking like a free person isn't just about addressing the false beliefs we struggle with, though I had quite a few of them. It's about fully embracing all God has for us, and more importantly, all God has already done for us. This is explained more fully in Freedom Step Five, but let me share how this pertains to our thought life.

I now know it doesn't matter how I feel; even if I feel rejected and abandoned, I am always in God's presence. In fact, Psalm 139 says there's nowhere I can go and *not* be in God's presence. I also now recognize that one of my default settings, a place I retreat to when triggered, is to feel rejected and abandoned.[14] Because I had experienced much rejection and abandonment in past relationships, I had unknowingly projected that onto my relationship with God, assuming He too would reject me as so many others had.

Another thing I'd cry out to God is, "God, why don't You speak to me? You must not like me, or I must have some unconfessed sin in my heart. So, God, I'm going to sit here until You either show me what that sin is or speak to me."

I was telling myself a half-truth, because the Bible does say in Psalm 66:18, "If I had cherished sin in my heart, the LORD would not have listened." I used that verse to beat myself up, as proof that I was a pile of sin and crud and that I couldn't hear from God because I had some cherished sin in my heart.

The truth of the matter is I was truly open to God's conviction. If you are honestly open to hearing from the Lord about any areas of sin or needed growth in your life, He will show them to you because He knows you were created for more; and He, like a good parent, desires that you experience all He has for you. In relationship, I don't need to constantly pester my close friends in order to find out if I've done something to offend or upset them. I trust we have the type of relationship where they will tell me if I've done something wrong. In the same way, I don't need to constantly look at my life with a magnifying glass, trying to figure out if I've somehow offended God or upset Him. There is always wisdom in praying as David prayed in Psalm 139, "Search me, O God … and see if there is any offensive way in me" (v.23). Notice it is God who is doing the searching, not we. This prayer is meant to be used as an open door to invite God in that He might speak and we might hear. We were not meant to pick through our day meticulously in hopes that we might find whatever cherished sin is keeping God from hearing our prayers.

Jesus said in John 10:27 (NASB), "My sheep hear My voice." Not "They might hear my voice," or "They could maybe one day hear my voice," or "If they really try hard," but "My sheep hear My voice." Period. The Bible is full of this type of promise—of what God has already done for believers and everything that is available to us simply because Jesus died on the cross.

If you're still allowing your old ways of thinking about yourself and about God to dictate your worth and your actions, you are basically telling Jesus that He's not allowed to be Lord of your life. You are accepting the salvation He is giving, but rejecting the transformation He is offering.

We need to allow Him to take His proper place—not only as the Savior of our souls, but also as Transformer of our lives and Redeemer and Renewer of our minds.

Read the following verse as you think about the things you have said to yourself recently:

> "Men will have to give account on the day of judg-
> ment for every careless word they have spoken."
> (Matthew 12:36)

You may have never thought to apply that verse to the words you say to yourself, but you are God's precious creation. If you are a believer in and follower of Jesus Christ, you have been adopted as God's child, God's beloved son or daughter. Think of how God's heart breaks when you speak cruelly to yourself.

I'm not a subscriber to "name it and claim it" theology, nor do I think we can speak anything we want into being. Those teachings take a truth of God to an extreme. That said, words do have power. Consider that with a word, God spoke the world into being. Consider that Jesus is the Word of God made flesh. Our words, even to ourselves, matter.

Think back to the last big mistake you made. Did you call yourself names? Did you curse yourself for taking a risk? Did you berate yourself for doing something "so stupid"?

I made a big blunder around the time I was first writing this. I was going through the chest freezer in our kitchen, pulling out food to defrost for that week's meals, and I left a bag of steaks on the floor when I put stuff back in the freezer. I didn't notice them there for over fifteen hours. These were no ordinary steaks. We had purchased a quarter of a grass-fed cow recently and split it with a friend. This was good quality meat, and now it was spoiled.

In the past, I would have taken the opportunity to berate myself, call myself names, and think about how stupid and scatter-brained I was for doing that. I would have gone through the list of reasons this was an awful mistake: our grocery bills are high already, another opportunity like this may not come along anytime soon, and now we have nothing for dinner.

How did I respond? I shrugged my shoulders, said, "Oh well," threw the bag in the trash, and went on with my day. I'm a human being, and I made a mistake. I didn't have to allow it to send me spiraling down into despair or to define my worth.

The book of Proverbs says, "Reckless words pierce like a sword" (12:18). A friend of mine used to say that words have the power to deposit courage into you (encourage) or rip courage out of you (discourage).[15]

How have your words to yourself been today? Have you been depositing courage into yourself by replacing the lies with truth or are you ripping courage out of yourself by mistaking the lies for truth?

Are you allowing your theology, your understanding of God's truth, to inform your experiences, or are you allowing your experiences alone to impact and change your beliefs? Stop and think about the difference. Are you looking at your experiences through the light of God's Word, or have you decided God's Word can't be fully true based on what you have experienced so far?

Abram (later called Abraham) had a promise from God that he would have a son (Genesis 15:4–5). Verse six says, "Abram believed the LORD, and he credited to him as righteousness." However, after a while, Abram's wife Sarai encouraged her husband to sleep with their servant, Hagar, and he did what she said. This was a common practice at that time, but this is not what God had told Abram to do. Rather than continuing to believe that God would be faithful to what He said He would do, Abram looked through the lens of his experience, seemingly decided it was taking God a long time to follow through, and chose to take matters into his own hands. Abram and Hagar had a son, Ishmael. Abram later did have the son of the promise with his wife and named him Isaac, but his choice to have a child with Hagar brought Abram much distress (you can read more in Genesis 15 and forward).

In Matthew 4, we read the account of Jesus being tempted after forty days of fasting. It was clear that Satan was lying and trying to mislead Jesus. Jesus could have just said, "Satan, you're ridiculous. Go away." Or worse, He could have given in to Satan's demands. He could have said, *I'm tired, and I'm hungry. God led me out here, I haven't eaten for 40 days, and Satan's been bothering me the whole time. His offer is pretty tempting right now. Who knows how long it will be before I get to eat again?* Instead, Jesus responded to Satan's lies with Scripture. Even in His tired, hungry state, as Satan selectively quoted Scripture to Jesus, Jesus had the Word so deep in His soul that it flowed right out of Him. When temptation and lies presented themselves, the truth was His natural response. He chose to take God at His Word.

How do we think like a free person? We need to think like Jesus. As I wrote in Freedom Step One, we need to immerse ourselves in God's Word. We can more easily recognize the lies when we have been soaked in truth.

Today, you have a choice. You can choose, through the Spirit, to begin to grasp, acknowledge, and believe what God has freely given to you. You can choose to trust that God is who He says He is. You can allow God, your source of life, to be the source of your thoughts. Invite Him to renew your mind as only He can. You can embrace all the promises the Word has for God's children. You can choose to attack the lies with truths from God's Word through the live-giving power of the Holy Spirit, who is able to guide you into all truth (John 16:13).

That's how free people think: Freedom Step Four.

FREEDOM STEP FIVE:
Act like a Free Person

PART OF LEARNING TO WALK IN FREEDOM is choosing to act like a free person.

2 Peter 1:3 says, "[Jesus'] divine power has given us everything we need for life and godliness."

The Bible reiterates this point in verses such as the following:

Galatians 5:24 says that those who belong to Christ Jesus have crucified the flesh (also called the sinful nature) with its passions and desires. It doesn't say "are in the process of crucifying the flesh" or "will someday master crucifying the flesh," but says the flesh has already been crucified.

Jesus Himself said in John 8:36, "So if the Son sets you free, you will be free indeed."

Galatians 5:13 says that the reason God called us was to be free, not so that we would struggle through life, just barely holding on till heaven.

Romans 6:6 says, "Knowing this, that our old self was crucified with Him, in order that our body of sin might be done away with, so that we would no longer be slaves to sin." (NASB) Verse 17 says we used to be slaves to sin, and verse 18 goes on to say that "You have been set free from sin and have become slaves to righteousness."

If this is really true—if, as believers, we are really free—this is really good news! Then why do we continue to act as if we are still enslaved to sin? Shouldn't it be easier, when we are faced with temptation, to just say no and walk away? Why, in Romans 7, directly after writing all these verses about not being a slave to sin, did Paul talk about his struggle with doing what he didn't want to do?

In fact, if we are already free—period, exclamation point, end of story—why do we even need the second half of the New Testament?

These are not questions I pose lightly. I shared in the introduction to this book how important it is to remember that freedom is both a one-time gift and a process. I also shared a glimpse into my own struggles with learning to walk in freedom. These are difficult questions, but the implications can be life-changing if we answer them accurately and choose to walk in the freedom those answers can offer.

So, why don't we act like free people?

In the circus, a common way to train an elephant is to tie him with strong ropes to a sturdy pole when he is young and small. He initially fights being tied to the pole, but eventually resigns himself to the fact that he cannot get free.

As the elephant grows, the pole and rope stay the same size. Though the animal has everything in him he needs in order to break free, he still acts as if he is in bondage to this pole and rope. The elephant is so used to being enslaved to the pole that he never tries to free himself.[16]

We believers often act the same way. We are so used to responding in a certain manner that we don't realize we can make different choices.

We can act like free people.

Let me share another analogy. Imagine that a person who has walked with a limp his whole life finds out there is a procedure available to correct that limp. He has the procedure, but he needs to undergo physical therapy to strengthen his weakened muscles. Because he has walked with a limp for so long, his muscles have actually conformed and adjusted to accommodate his limp.

He needs to relearn how to walk.[17]

As individuals, we should not be surprised that we often walk with a limp. All of humanity walks with the same limp. Yet, as believers, we have the opportunity to walk in freedom through Christ's work on the cross and the power of the Holy Spirit.

We can proactively make choices to act like the free people that we already are.

That said, there is an issue with what many of us might think it looks like to act like a free person, or what freedom really is. We believe that God wants us to behave better than we are. The Bible talks about behavior, right? We know God wants us to do certain things and doesn't want us to do others. So, we exert our effort on solely gathering knowledge about what God wants in an attempt to behave as we believe God wants us to.

I am not saying that gathering knowledge is wrong. There is plenty of quality literature written by Christians that can shed light on our lives and struggles. I participated in many book studies that had a profound effect on my life. I also shared the power that can be found in knowing the Word of God. So what is the danger of simply gathering knowledge?

Say you have a struggle with pornography. You know you shouldn't view it. In fact, you get even further convicted when, after having an extended Saturday porn marathon, you go to church on Sunday, and the pastor preaches on the dangers of pornography and the objectification it entails. You go to the altar, you repent as best you know how, you might even ask someone to pray for you with some vague sharing like, "I just feel God speaking to me and need prayer."

Then you go home and tell God you're going to change. This is the end of the road for that struggle; you're not going to do it again. You might even read some books on why pornography is bad, how the industry treats the workers, how viewing porn enslaves a person, and 10 tips on overcoming. And motivated by this gathering of knowledge, you keep trying harder.

Then you likely fail again.

This is basically what I did, as briefly described in Freedom Step Three. I would feel genuinely convicted about something. I would be truly grieved by my sin and exhausted by the insanity the cycle of sin produced in my life. I would gather books, Bible studies and articles to help me understand the struggles, and I would try and use that knowledge to inspire myself to better behavior.

I had sincere intentions and my heart was certainly in the right place, but I was going about it the wrong way.

So, how then should a free person act?

A free person actively overcomes life-controlling issues by becoming plugged in to the power source and remaining plugged in.

In doing a search in the New Testament for the word *power*, I noticed that Luke, in the gospel he wrote, talks about power more than the other three gospels combined. He talks about Jesus doing what He did under the power of the Holy Spirit.

The other book Luke wrote, the book of Acts, is short for the Acts of the Apostles, but it might more accurately be named the Acts of the Holy Spirit. In the beginning of the book of Acts, Jesus tells the apostles to wait in Jerusalem, because "you will receive power when the Holy Spirit comes on you" (Acts 1:8). Luke saw this power, the power of the Holy Spirit, up close and experienced it intimately. He saw its importance. He recorded the difference it made in the lives of the disciples, including Peter, who on the day of Pentecost, when the Holy Spirit came upon them in Jerusalem, shared the hope of Jesus Christ with the crowds, and 3,000 people believed and were baptized.

God is meant to be our source of power. Through His Holy Spirit given to us as believers, we can be empowered to make better choices, but what we often try to do is take our knowledge and our will power and use them as our source of power for overcoming our struggles.

Bob Hamp gives this analogy.[18] It's like taking the Ethernet cable (which connects your computer to the Internet) and plugging it into the spot for the power cord. We try to take data, the knowledge we have gathered, and use that to fuel our obedience. We attempt to derive power from data or knowledge rather than the power God offers.

I don't think we do this through a conscious decision. It is often just a habit. It is how we were taught to achieve in other areas of our lives. When we weren't successful the first time, we were encouraged to try again—only this time, try harder! And so we try again to behave well, but this time, we try harder.

The problem with this approach is we forget we didn't come to God on our own strength in the first place. There is nothing we did to deserve or earn our salvation or our adoption as God's children. As Galatians 3:3 states clearly, why would we begin in the Spirit and then try "to become perfect by your own human effort" (NLT)?

I quoted 2 Peter 1:3 earlier: "His divine power has given us everything we need for life and godliness." Imagine that we, as believers in Jesus, are like a lamp. That lamp has everything in it that it needs in order to function as it was created to: electrical wires, functioning light bulbs, and a switch to turn it on, but if I do not plug the lamp into the electrical outlet, it won't work.

In the Garden of Eden, not only did we become disconnected from our source of life, we became disconnected from our source of power. That power enters back into us when we become believers, as every believer receives the Holy Spirit, but we need to continually reconnect.

That doesn't mean the Holy Spirit comes and goes completely as He often did in the Old Testament accounts, where we read about the Holy Spirit coming upon people only temporarily so they can prophesy or be empowered for leadership or a particular event. The Holy Spirit always dwells in believers. Yet Paul commands the Ephesus church to be "filled with the Holy Spirit" (Ephesians 5:18, NASB). Why would Paul be telling believers to be filled with the Spirit? They already had the Holy Spirit in them. We can gather from the passage that we need to "keep being filled." The passage shows us that the filling of the Spirit is something we need to continually seek and ask for.

I stated in Freedom Step Three that Jesus didn't die just to modify our behavior. Yes, the Bible does have guidelines for our behavior. Just as good parents give their children boundaries to live by, so does God. However, let us consider both why God gives us these guidelines and what our motivation for following them should be.

I shared earlier that I'm a mother. At this writing, I have 2 sons under the age of 6. I tell my children not to touch the hot stove, because I don't want them to experience the pain of being burned. I ask them to hold my hand when they cross the street, because I am more aware of the dangers involved than they are and am able to be more alert and observant of potential harm. I ask them to be kind to their parents, each other, and others, because they'd like to be treated kindly themselves.

When they do not listen or obey, I do not withdraw my acceptance of them. I do not withhold my love from them because they made choices contrary to my teachings. Instead, my heart breaks that they now have experienced a type of pain I hoped they could avoid. Even though they were disobedient, I still rush in to comfort them in their pain. We talk later, outside of the moment, about the cause and effect that was put into action when they disobeyed. We also discuss how they could make different choices next time.

Through all of that, they are still my children, and I would proudly say so, even in their disobedience. As a perfect parent, God says the same and more. Before Jesus accomplished anything noteworthy enough to include in the Bible, God proudly declared, "This is my Son, whom I love; with Him I am well pleased" (Matthew 3:17).[19] I say the same of my children. He is my child, whom I love dearly. He is human. He will make mistakes. He will be imperfect, just as I am imperfect. I can model how to forgive, ask for forgiveness, and make different choices in the future.

God does not want to see us harmed. He urges us "to present [our] bodies a living and holy sacrifice, acceptable to God, *which is* [our] spiritual service of worship" (Romans 12:1, NASB). He reassures us that "whoever finds his life will lose it, and whoever loses his life for my sake will find it" (Matthew 10:39).

Has obedience become a dirty word in today's church culture? I can understand the tendency to avoid it. Out of various church movements of the 19th and 20th century arose much legalism. Lots of rules were enacted to measure "good Christian behavior." I did something similar in my life. I was trying to "white knuckle" my way to holiness with Brenna's Rules for Good Christian Living.

The backlash against legalism has been to more fully embrace grace (which I agree with), but now, it seems behavior is talked about much less. Pastors are afraid to stand in the pulpit or even sit in their offices and say, "This behavior is not God's best for your life," for fear of offending someone.

Where's the balance? If it's true that God's grace empowers us, if it's true that we are clothed in God's righteousness, how are we to live? How are we to act like free people?

When I left behind homosexual relationships in March of 2000, I made a choice. I chose to walk in obedience to what I believed God said in His Word about my sexuality.

Did choosing to obey make me more free? This is a question I have really wrestled with. If Jesus came to set us free through Spirit-empowered living, what part did my choices play?

We can ask the question from the opposite angle. If I had chosen instead to continue to walk in disobedience to God, would that have helped me learn to walk in freedom? Certainly not. Romans 6:16 (NLT) says, "Don't you realize that you become the slave of whatever you choose to obey?"

We can choose to obey God, not because we are concerned that His love for us is conditional, but out of a trust that He has our best interest in mind. We can obey, because we believe He has good things for us.

When I began to walk in obedience, I obeyed God because I was afraid of His rejection. I thought His feelings were as fickle as mine: that if I made good choices, He loved me and was pleased with me, but if I made bad choices, He was immediately furious and turned His back on me.

That is not the character of God. God said about Himself to Moses:

> "The LORD, the LORD, the compassionate and gracious
> God, slow to anger, abounding in love and faithfulness,
> maintaining love to thousands, and forgiving wickedness,
> rebellion and sin." (Exodus 34:6–7)

That's the forgiving, loving, patient God I now know and try to love with all that I am. "We love because he first loved us" (1 John 4:19). I can now obey Him out of a place of love and a deep recognition of all He did to give me life. Jesus showed His love and obedience to God His Father by praying, "Yet not as I will, but as you will." He then followed His Father obediently when He allowed Himself to be nailed to a cross (Matthew 26:39). One way to show my love is through obedience.

Jesus also said, "If you love me, you will obey what I command" (John 14:15). Depending on your background, when you read that passage, you may hear: *If I loved God, I would obey Him perfectly, but since I don't, I must not really love Him.* This is what I hear, through the filter of knowing God as patient, kind, and abounding in love and faithfulness: *If I fully love God with all that I have and all that I am, out of that heart of love and trust will flow obedience because I know of His goodness and faithfulness.*

Jesus goes on immediately to talk about the Holy Spirit. This is not a coincidence. Verses 16 and 17 say,

> "And I will ask the Father, and he will give you another
> Counselor to be with you forever—the Spirit of truth.
> The world cannot accept him, because it neither sees him
> nor knows him. But you know him, for he lives with you
> and will be in you."

God gave us the Holy Spirit to help us to love Him fully and to empower us to obey His commands. He sent us His Spirit so we can then act like the free person He already made us to be.

How do we act like a free person? We all have those moments where we are tempted to act like our old self and not like a free person, those moments where we are:

- Tempted to sin
- Tempted to see ourselves in any other way than how God sees us, and act accordingly
- Tempted to believe the lies we have bought into and fall back into old patterns
- Tempted to take our unhealthy and unhelpful thoughts and run with them

A free person grows to realize the temptation she is experiencing is common to human beings (1 Corinthians 10:13). That person chooses to act as if she were free rather than act as if she were still enslaved to that temptation and had to give in.

A free person would say to that lie about his identity, "That's not what Jesus says about me!" A free person would say to that boundary violation, "I will leave the room if you continue to speak to me that way."[20] A free person would reason, "In the past when my emotions have felt overwhelming, rather than choose to feel them, I chose to medicate my emotions through food, sex, power, escape. I can make different choices today, knowing that I can experience these emotions and they won't suffocate me, because I can handle anything through the power of the Holy Spirit, with the Freedom Giver and other freedom seekers at my side."

This isn't just about saying no to sin, though that is an important piece. It's about saying *no* to bondage in all its forms and saying *yes* to learning to walk in freedom.

We are training to run a new race. When we were slaves to sin, our body and mind were trained, when faced with temptation, to respond a certain way. We gave in to the negative thoughts, we let our boundaries be trampled on, and we believed the lies we'd been told. An athlete needs to discipline himself to train, when it might feel more natural to sit on the couch and watch TV. We, too, need to train and discipline ourselves so that when we are faced with temptation, we, like Joseph in Genesis 39, flee the scene rather than stay in a tempting situation.

From now on, think of it this way: Sin speaks a dead
language that means nothing to you; God speaks your
mother tongue, and you hang on every word. You are
dead to sin and alive to God. That's what Jesus did. That
means *you must not give sin a vote in the way you conduct
your lives.* Don't give it the time of day. Don't even run
little errands that are connected with that old way of life.
Throw yourselves wholeheartedly and full-time—
remember, you've been raised from the dead!—into God's
way of doing things. Sin can't tell you how to live. After
all, you're not living under that old tyranny any longer.
You're living in the freedom of God. (Romans 6:11–14,
MSG, emphasis mine)

There are a million different reasons we choose to give in to old patterns of behavior rather than choosing to act free. It's not just because it
feels good or natural. For many of us, these old ways of responding are all
we have ever known. We may have begun self-medicating with various
behaviors at a young age, because we lacked coping mechanisms to deal
with the painful trials in our lives. We wanted to escape uncomfortable
feelings. This continued as adults. We felt lonely, rejected, or unlovable—so
we went out and tried to hook up with someone. We overate. We overspent.
We fantasized. The feelings were still there, but we got to avoid them for a
while. We may have felt entitled to the temporary pleasure and relief of sin,
telling ourselves, *I deserve this.* Sometimes, it's simply habit. It's become the
way we are, and what we've always done.

Except it's not the way we are anymore! If we are in Christ, we are now
slaves to righteousness (Romans 6:18). We have the capacity and ability,
through the power of the Holy Spirit, to make different choices.

When we start actively saying no to our old nature and way of doing
things, we need to make sure we have our support system in place to help
us follow through (back to Freedom Step Two) and to hold us accountable. I heard someone who struggled with same-sex attraction share in
his testimony that he would go to his counseling appointments, feel all
these overwhelming feelings, and on the way home, he'd hook up with
someone. Finally, he contacted a friend and said something to the effect of,
"Look, I just need someone to hang out with me for a couple hours after
my appointment."[21] He recognized a pattern in his life and addressed it by

expressing his needs. Learning to voice your wants and needs is necessary to overcome. And learning to sit with those uncomfortable feelings, turning them continually over to God, is also part of learning to walk in freedom.

Acting like a free person is possible through the power of the Holy Spirit. A free person chooses to obey God out of love and knows that he can boldly approach God's throne, where grace and mercy are freely available to him whenever he needs it (Hebrews 4:16).

That is how a free person acts: Freedom Step Five.

CONCLUSION

THIS LIST OF FIVE FREEDOM STEPS is by no means exhaustive, nor is it intended to be formulaic. They are simply some truths that have helped me and others as we desire to walk in the fullness of all that Jesus died to give us.

We cannot find true healing, nor can we grow into who God created us to be, without God breathing life into these five freedom steps.

We need to be willing to do whatever it takes to walk in freedom. Whatever it takes! If you struggle with pornography, put a filter on your computer, or install Covenant Eyes or a similar software, which reports the sites you view to the accountability people in your life.

Can't think of anyone to hold you accountable? Then disconnect the Internet at your house or on your phone. Go to the library to check your email.

You may be thinking, "Now, that's just unrealistic." Remember, we lived for centuries without e-mail, and even as recently as 10 or 15 years ago, it was something only a few people could access from their homes. Some people still don't have email. Shocking, I know! I recently got a phone with Internet access, and now I wonder how I ever lived without it, but if having Internet on my phone began to challenge my ability to walk in freedom, I'd get rid of it in a second.

Some people I know can't even watch secular TV, because the themes are triggers for them. Others cannot listen to certain types of music, because of the emotional roller coaster onto which it sends them. I struggle with overeating, and there are times I've had to stop eating a certain item because I can't seem to practice self-control around those foods. Given I had an eating disorder for 13 years, I used to think freedom in this area meant the ability to practice self-control around all food. But does an alcoholic keep alcohol around for the sole purpose of testing her self-control? No, that doesn't make sense. So if secular TV or sharp cheddar cheese causes you to stumble, you might consider Jesus' instructions to "cut it off and throw it away" (Matthew 5:30).

Those are drastic measures. You may not need to do any of those things, but God calls us to surrender all to Him. Sometimes, that involves doing whatever it takes to become the free people we already are. Only we can evaluate what "whatever it takes" is, with the help of freedom seekers around us, as well as the direction of the Freedom Giver and the Holy Spirit, who guides us into all truth (John 16:13).

> "Whoever finds his life will lose it, and whoever loses his
> life for my sake will find it." (Matthew 10:39)

These all may simply seem like behavior modification. As you may know, you can modify your behavior without really being free. However, these are some potential ways to set yourself up for success as you allow God to teach you to walk in freedom. It would be cruel to hand my child a lollipop and then tell him not to eat it. Why would you have known stumbling blocks in your environment if you didn't have to?

We need to take baby steps. If you're unwilling to take even a baby step in the direction of healing, then you don't really want freedom in your life.

At a conference, I heard a speaker share that she made a list of 20 people she could call if she was having a moment of temptation. She wrote the list in order of how well she knew these people, #1 being her closest friend and #20 being a good acquaintance. One day during such a moment, she called through the entire list. No one answered. She started calling through the list again. #14 picked up. She said something like, "I'm calling because I'm struggling with temptation right now and just needed to tell someone. Could you pray with me, and then ask me tomorrow if I made good choices for the rest of the day?" She didn't need to go into details, but she needed to reach out and be honest with someone.[22]

I remember being at an event, where an ex-girlfriend made it very clear she would like to get back together. As soon as I got home, I called a friend and let her know what happened, lest I be tempted to respond (and I was). It was one or two in the morning, but I didn't care (and I had my friend's permission to call her at any time, if needed). My relationship with God and my walk toward freedom were just that important. I had come a long way, but I took 1 Corinthians 10:12 to heart, knowing that despite my resolution to stand firm, I was not above making a poor choice.

You may be thinking, *That's fine for you, Brenna, but you don't know how dirty and ugly my struggles are.* Perhaps you've convinced yourself that you can't tell anyone, that no one would understand, or that you're too embarrassed or ashamed about the details of your struggles to bring accountability into your life. Those things may feel true to you, but they are lies from the enemy. His main message is shaming, and it's designed to keep you bound. You are in essence saying that you are unwilling to do what God says is necessary for walking in freedom.

I do get it; I know how hard it can be to open up. Not only did I struggle with same-sex attraction for years, I had an eating disorder in which I was addicted to laxatives (talk about gross) and I self-injured. I cut myself with anything I could get my hands on, and when I decided that was just not acceptable (too many scars), I punched things, punched myself and banged my head against walls.

That's some pretty ugly stuff. And that's just the beginning.

I also understand that there may be serious ramifications of your honesty, such as possible loss of relationship. But I came to the point where I had to stop being so concerned about people's opinions of me, or what might happen if I opened up. I *could not* live this way anymore—my desire for experiencing freedom in my life began to outweigh any shame or embarrassment I felt. The bottom line was I was tired of struggling; I knew there must be more than this. I became more disgusted by the bondage in my life than I was concerned about what anyone thought of me.

I need to be willing to walk out Hebrews 12:1-3.

> Let us throw off everything that hinders and the sin that
> so easily entangles, and let us run with perseverance the
> race marked out for us. Let us fix our eyes on Jesus, the
> author and perfecter of our faith, who for the joy set
> before him endured the cross, scorning its shame, and sat
> down at the right hand of the throne of God. Consider
> him who endured such opposition from sinful men, so
> that you will not grow weary and lose heart.

Free people do whatever it takes to become free and remain free. *Whatever it takes.* Jesus did whatever it took so we have the opportunity to learn to walk in freedom. He gave up everything as He hung from that cross, dying a criminal's death, carrying the sin and the shame of the entire world on His back.

It's OK to be not quite there yet. When I started to recover from my eating disorder, I prayed, "God, help me want to recover." I knew the reality of recovery: that it would be difficult and lengthy, that I would gain weight, and that I would have to deal with all the pain and hurt I was trying to avoid by abusing my body. I didn't want that. Who would? So I prayed, "God, help me to want recovery. Help me desire You."

The reality of life is that there will always be challenges. I recently heard someone who lost over 100 pounds and kept it off for several years say this, "Being overweight is hard, losing weight is hard, and maintaining your weight loss is hard. Choose your hard." I absolutely love that! Walking in freedom is challenging, period. So is walking around, still in bondage. Surrendering our lives to Jesus and walking in obedience is difficult. But it can also be full of joy, peace, and freedom like we never dreamed possible. Choose your hard.

God gave His only Son for you, for your freedom. Tasting freedom will eventually be so much more satisfying than a life of bondage. God wants us to experience true freedom, the freedom that is available to all of us through the resurrection power of Jesus Christ. He desires that you become the person He created you to be. He longs to see His children learn to walk in freedom.

Pray this with me:

> *God, you know where my heart is today. You know the doubts and the fears and the struggles. Help me desire freedom. Give me the willingness to do whatever it takes to follow You and to experience all You have for me. Help me recognize the lies and replace them with truth. Forgive me for not relying on Your grace, but instead relying on my own strength and effort. Forgive me for my unwillingness to take drastic measures, for making excuses, for hiding from You and Your healing and love. I need You. Your Word says when I am weak, You are strong and that in Your strength,*

I can do all things. I need You. I desperately need You. Let Your Spirit fill me, empower me, and renew me again. Be Lord of my life today and every day. In Jesus' mighty, powerful, holy name, I pray. Amen.

STUDY QUESTIONS

THE FOLLOWING STUDY QUESTIONS, arranged by chapter, may help with further study. I also list the scriptures referenced in each section so you can review them again.

Preface

Scriptures referenced: 2 Corinthians 5:17, Matthew 11:28–30

Introduction to Freedom

Scriptures referenced: Luke 4:18, Galatians 5:1, 13, Luke 1:37, Romans 6:17–18, 2 Peter 1:3, John 8:36, Galatians 5:13, 1 John 3:9, John 3:16, John 10:10, Genesis 1:26–27, Genesis 2:7, 2 Corinthians 5:19

1. When you have considered freedom in the past, what did you think it would look like?

2. In what ways can freedom be both a one-time gift and a process? Go back and read the analogy used there of a marathon athlete (pg.13). Does that make sense to you?

3. Having read this introduction, what would true freedom look like in your own life? What are you hoping for?

4. Why do you believe Jesus came to earth?

5. Think about how God was Adam and Eve's source prior to the eating of the fruit. Who or what is your source? From where do you draw life? Where do you run in times of trial and stress? Straight to God in prayer? Or to food, sex, TV, shopping, or some other means of escape?

Freedom Step One:

Spend Time with the Freedom Giver

Scriptures referenced: James 1:13, 1 Corinthians 6:9–11, Psalm
139:13–14, Psalm 50:21, Psalm 139:7-10, Psalm 34:18, Psalm
34:10, Psalm 86:15, James 1:5, James 1:22, Matthew 10:29–31,
Matthew 25:40, Revelation 2:1–6, 1 Peter 4:11, Psalm 46:10,
Matthew 7:22–23, Matthew 7:9, Psalm 119:45, James 4:8a

1. At your core, what do you believe about God and His character?
   One way to answer this question is to recognize the things about
   God that you believe to be true and pray for in others' lives, but do
   not fully believe for yourself.

2. How would you say your relationship with God is today? Close?
   Distant? Strong? Turbulent? Needs work?

3. If you don't spend regular time with God, what is keeping you
   from doing so?

4. Look up one of the above Scriptures and read it in context, open
   to whatever part of the Bible you are reading through currently,
   or read a portion of Scripture that is a favorite of yours. Take the
   time to listen to and learn about God's heart. If there's something
   you don't understand or can't make sense of, ask Him for help. Ask
   God, through His Holy Spirit, to reveal His heart to you.

5. Do you practice silence and solitude? How has it been helpful?
   Challenging?

6. Psalm 138:2 says, "I praise your name for your unfailing love and
   faithfulness; for your promises are backed by all the honor of your
   name" (NLT). Pause for a minute and consider how your life would
   be changed if you consistently took God at His Word. Discuss this
   with others.

Freedom Step Two:
Spend Time with Freedom Seekers

Scriptures referenced: Hebrews 10:24–25, 2 Corinthians 12:8, Acts 2:42–44, Matthew 28:19–20, James 5:16, 1 John 1:5, John 11:1–44, 2 Corinthians 12:9-10, John 6, Matthew 17, Luke 8, Mark 14

1. Read through John 11:1–44. If you are familiar with the story, pick up a translation of the Bible that you are not familiar with. (The NASB, MSG, or NLT are some good options.) If you don't have another translation of the Bible handy, go to Biblegateway.com to find one. Pause and reflect for a moment. Consider taking some notes. What do you learn about community in these passages? What do you learn about the character of God as Jesus interacts with Lazarus, his sisters and with the crowds?

2. How are your relationships today? Do you feel you have the support you need to learn to walk in freedom? If the answer is no, what steps can you take to find support?

3. How are you supporting and serving others?

4. Starting with "Remember first that no one is 'normal'", there are some suggestions on how to cultivate healthy relationships (beginning on pg. 32). Which one do you need to work on?

5. If you needed accountability today, who would you call? Do you have anyone? If not, consider asking a leader at your church if there is anyone who might be willing to help in this way.

Freedom Step Three:
Embrace Grace

Scriptures referenced: Hebrews 4:16, Galatians 3:1–3, Colossians 2:20–23, Romans 12:2, Luke 1:30; 2:40; 2:52, John 1:14, 16–17, Ephesians 4:7, 2 Timothy 2:1, Acts 6:8, Acts 7:46, James 4:6-7, 2 Corinthians 12:8–10

1. How would you define grace? What have you been taught about

grace in the past?

2. To what degree have you struggled with legalism?

3. There are many Scriptures referenced in this Freedom Step. Select a few and read those verses in context. Once again, consider using a different translation that you are less familiar with. What do those verses tell you about grace?

4. What does it mean to embrace grace?

5. What aspect of grace—*charis*—do you most need in your life today?

Freedom Step Four:

Think like a Free Person

Scriptures referenced: Proverbs 23:7, Romans 12:2, John 8:44, 2 Corinthians 10:4–5, Philippians 4:19, Psalm 34:10, Luke 12:7, Matthew 7:9, Mark 9:24, Psalm 139, Psalm 66:18, Psalm 139:23, John 10:27, Matthew 12:36, Proverbs 12:18, Genesis 15:4–6, Matthew 4, John 16:13

1. Reflect on 2 Corinthians 10:4–5. Grab a different translation. Put the text into your own words. Focus on key words and themes. What does this verse have to say about thinking like a free person?

2. Have you noticed any thought patterns in yourself that aren't helpful and keep you bound?

3. How well are you able to recognize your negative thought patterns? What does it mean for you to "take them captive"?

4. How are your words to yourself? Encouraging (depositing courage in you) or discouraging (ripping courage out of you)?

5. Stop for a minute and pray. Take some deep breaths. Ask God to show you the areas where you have chosen to believe the lies of the enemy. Ask the Holy Spirit to renew your mind with the truth of who God says you are.

Freedom Step Five:
Act like a Free Person

Scriptures referenced: 2 Peter 1:3, Galatians 5:24, John 8:36, Galatians 5:13, Romans 6:6, 17–18, Romans 7:14–20, Acts 1:8, Galatians 3:3, 2 Peter 1:3, Ephesians 5:18, Matthew 3:17, Romans 12:1, Matthew 10:39, Romans 6:16, Exodus 34:6–7, 1 John 4:19, Matthew 26:39, John 14:15–17, 1 Corinthians 10:13, Genesis 39:12, Romans 6:11–14, Romans 6:18, Hebrews 4:16

1. What is your "limp"? Do you have a struggle that continually trips you up, or an area of your life where you do not act like a free person?

2. Do you have habits that are negatively impacting you? Areas of your life where you need to set boundaries?

3. Re-read the analogies and examples of using knowledge as your power source versus using the Holy Spirit to empower you to act like a free person (pp. 51–53). Pray and ask God to reveal to you areas where you have been trying to achieve obedience in your own strength.

4. As a Christian, would you describe yourself as obedient or disobedient? Why? What are your motives for obedience? Is obedience a challenging word for you to consider?

5. What has helped you achieve sustained obedience in the past?

6. When you struggle with sin, do you ask for God's help? How could you invite the Holy Spirit to empower you?

Conclusion

Scriptures referenced: Matthew 5:30, John 16:13, Matthew 10:39, 1 Corinthians 10:12 , Hebrews 12:1–3

1. Reflect on John 5:1–7 and ask yourself, "Do you want to get well?" You'll notice in verse seven the sick man lists several reasons why he couldn't get in the pool, but he did not directly answer Jesus' yes or no question. If you answered "yes," that you want to get well, then ask yourself if you are willing to do what it takes to learn

to walk in freedom. Take this to prayer and consider journaling about your answer.

2. Read Matthew 10:39 again. Are there areas of your life that you have not released to God? Pause to ask God to reveal anything you might be holding on to.

3. Review the five Freedom Steps. Which one feels the most pressing to you right now? What action can you take to work on that? Who in your life can hold you accountable to that action? Call or email that person and set up a face-to-face meeting to discuss this accountability.

MY TESTIMONY

I HAVE GIVEN many different versions of my testimony throughout the years. I chose this one because throughout *Learning to Walk in Freedom* the emphasis is on our words and our thoughts. I pray you are blessed by this sharing of the work God has done in me. To Him be the glory.

A Christian speaker recently reminded me that words are a container for power. The book of Proverbs says "reckless words pierce like a sword," "the words of the wicked lie in wait for blood," and "when words are many, sin is not absent." In the Bible, names are very important. Throughout my life, I allowed people and circumstances to label me, name me, and define who I am.

I was born prematurely in May of 1975. I was given a 50% chance of survival and shipped off to a hospital 50 miles away since the hospital where I was born did not have facilities to care for those born prematurely. My mother was not allowed to ride with me. I was born without a name.

My parents didn't know if I would be male or female, and certainly weren't expecting my arrival almost two months early. I spent the next two months isolated in an incubator. During that time, premature babies were not touched or held. I was so sick that they ran out of places to stick needles, and had to have my head shaved on the sides for more needle ports. The names I picked up were: abandoned, rejected, unloved, shameful, worthy of pain—as good as dead.

My mother is an alcoholic and when she would drink, she would recount those days, saying, "You were bought from hell." What she was trying to express to me was the trauma of my birth and the extreme circumstances I was rescued out of. What I heard, from my already broken filter, was: inconvenient, bothersome, a burden.

As a child, I even remember being hyper-focused on the lyrics to the songs my parents listened to: "I got some news for you and you'll soon find out it's true. And you'll have to eat your lunch all by yourself" and "Hide your head in the sand, little girl, that's the end, little girl." I'd zero in on themes of abandonment, and I carried those feelings of fear with me into adulthood. I heard: be on your guard, you will be rejected and alone.

During my youth, my family attended liberal churches, serving on various committees and singing in choirs. I'd always believed in God, but it had little effect on my daily life. My mother continued to drink, ranting at me about the evils of men, what a bad child I was, and seemingly favoring my sister. What I heard: I was not worth protecting, the castaway, again a burden.

I began experimenting sexually with girls at a young age. This continued until, as a high school freshman, I found myself physically attracted to my best friend. We began a sexual relationship. I also developed an eating disorder and a struggle with self-injury. About a week into my high school relationship, I secretly looked up "homosexuality" in a health book. The book said that if you had attractions for someone of the same gender, then you were gay. I remember thinking, "There it is, in black and white. I am a homosexual." I already felt: unlovable, out of control, too much and now a dyke.

The summer after my high school graduation, I was asked if I was interested in going to church with someone I met in a coffee shop. The church was quick to tell me that homosexuality was a sin that would condemn me to hell. Every night I would cry myself to sleep, praying, "God, change me! Why did you make me gay if that means I have to go to hell? Is it true that You want me to be forever separated from You?" The church I was attending did not share the hope for change that the gospel offers to those struggling with same-sex attraction. Their stance was change first —then God will accept you. I decided I had asked God to change me, and He didn't. And so I embraced my lesbian identity, all the while the labels were being reinforced: rejected, abandoned, unheard, miniscule, unlovable—even by God.

After three and a half years together, my first girlfriend and I broke up. I then met an older married woman, dropped out of college and moved across the country to live with her and her husband. She and I had a mock wedding ceremony and from then on, she introduced me as her "wife." I lived with this couple for close to two and a half years. My "wife" paraded me around almost like a trophy. When she suggested I have sex with her husband, I did. I had never been with a man before. Even after she decided she no longer wanted her husband having sex with me, he would sneak into my room in the middle of the night while I tried to press myself up against the wall and hide. The names kept coming: worthless, voiceless, ashamed, only good for one thing: sex.

My "wife" and I eventually decided it would be best for me to continue my schooling, so I moved to Boston to attend a prestigious music school, the same school from which my "wife" had graduated. Though I was in an environment where my sexuality was affirmed, I was far from happy. My relationship with my "wife" continued to crumble until she ended our relationship about 10 months after I moved. My eating disorder spiraled out of control. I was afraid and alone.

Christians seemed to pop into my life to pray for me. They never took it upon themselves to point out my sinfulness or say that I should not be a lesbian. They just pointed me to Jesus. Like everyone else, I was a sinner in need of Jesus in my life. My sexual choices were only some of many indications of this need.

Things continued to worsen. I knew that I needed help with my eating disorder, or I was going to die, but I felt I had tried everything and nothing worked. A friend in recovery suggested I try to pray. I thought, "That's the one thing I haven't tried!"—so I started praying.

Around this time, a friend gave me a music CD by a passionate Christian artist. One night while listening, the words of a song gripped my heart. I felt completely alone. The man sang of a friend who was always there, with every tear cried, a friend who would give everything for him. That friend was Jesus—the son of God, who died on the cross to take away my sin, my pain, the false labels I had taken on, and to declare my worth. In the midst of that song, I cried out to God saying, "I want what he has!" God, in His great mercy, met me on that day in January of 1999. I felt: hopeful.

But the names did not disappear. I began to feel doomed to a life where I would carry those labels forever. Even though at the time I could not voice what was going on, I continued to spiral out of control with my eating and relationships. I was so desperate for love that I entered into a relationship with an 18 year old woman with a drug problem (I was 24 at the time).

After three months, this woman (having been raised in a Christian home) said to me, "Listen—the Bible says you must either be hot or cold—one or the other, but not both. You can't be a Christian and be gay." And with that, she ended our relationship.

I threw up my arms saying, "Fine, God! I don't want to live like this. Please take this away from me." In many ways, He did. My attraction to women greatly lessened, but the circumstances of my life that led me in the direction of lesbianism had not changed. I felt unsure, but truly desperate for God.

I didn't know that support groups existed when I was struggling. I opened up to my Christian friends about my struggle and asked for accountability. The labels were still haunting me. I needed more help. I found a Christian counselor who helped me to deal with my same-sex attraction, as well as my depression, self-injury, and my eating disorder, which had continued to rage out of control. Romans 12:2 (NLT) says, "Let God transform you into a new person by changing the way you think." The labels reminded me that I truly needed my entire thought life to be transformed. It wasn't that I had moments of feeling worthless and unlovable; in the core of my being, I was sure it was true. My counselor helped me to recognize these faulty names I had allowed to attach to me and showed me how to make them line up with what God's Word has to say about me (2 Corinthians 10:5). She helped me to trust in who the Bible says God is.

My counselor also helped me to see that I had attached all sorts of labels and names to God, most of them not true or not accurate: unreachable, unloving, distant, unconcerned with my life and struggles, nitpicky, only interested in my failures, punitive, impatient, and constantly angry. So I wrestled with God. In all honesty, I suppose, it was more like I wrestled and He waited patiently for me to realize that He is who He says He is and He will do what He has said He will do. In the Gospel of John, chapter 6, Jesus gave the disciples a particularly difficult command. Rather than trusting Jesus, quite a few of the disciples decided to stop following Christ. When Jesus asked the Twelve if they would leave too, Peter responded, "Master, to whom would we go? You have the words of real life, eternal life. We've already committed ourselves, confident that you are the Holy One of God" (v.68–69, MSG). That's how I felt. In the midst of all the questions and doubts, I already knew that I had tasted and seen that the Lord is indeed good.

A few months after surrendering my sexuality to God, I met a man through the campus ministry we both attended. Roy and I continued to be friends for five months, at which time we began dating. It wasn't always an easy relationship. The grip the names had on me was loosening—but it was very slow and painful.

When we first became friends, I was drawn to his strong faith, his free spirit and love for life. I can see that my lack of physical attraction to men in general was due in part to my fear of men and the lies my mother had instilled in me. As I learned more about Roy, as I grew to trust him, and as I recognized that he wouldn't hurt me, my natural physical attraction was allowed to surface without fear.

Roy and I have been married for over 10 years and have two beautiful sons. Marriage is not a cure for homosexuality, or a guarantee of happiness, but simply another part of God's healing process in my life. I thank God that I came to a point where in my heart of hearts, I felt I had no choice but to embrace Christ and all that He required of me. But what I got in return for my obedience and hard work is an amazing godly man who loves me, unconditionally, like no woman ever did.

I also needed to allow God to give me new names. Rather than feeling unlovable at my core, I know that my Father calls me beloved, cherished. I now embrace the truth that the apostle John knew well: that as a believer, I am God's favorite (John 13:3).[23] Rather than being ashamed of who I am and who I was, God calls me precious, beautiful, redeemed—He has borne my shame. He calls me worth knowing, worth loving and worth creating. I am mighty in Him, delightful, created in my Father's image and strong when I am weak. And in those moments when I feel abandoned, I remember there is nowhere I can go to flee from God's presence, and when I feel rejected, I know I will never have to feel the rejection that my Savior felt as He hung from that cross. And my mother was right in one of the things she told me: I was bought from hell—not only eternally, but today, God has given me abundant life and a true freedom I never knew could be possible.

What names have you allowed to speak death to you?

Isaiah 62:1–4 says,

> For Zion's sake I will not keep silent,
>> for Jerusalem's sake I will not remain quiet,
> till her vindication shines out like the dawn,

> her salvation like a blazing torch.
> The nations will see your vindication,
>> and all kings your glory;
> you will be called by a new name
>> that the mouth of the LORD will bestow.
> You will be a crown of splendor in the LORD's hand,
>> a royal diadem in the hand of your God.
> No longer will they call you Deserted,
>> or name your land Desolate.
> But you will be called Hephzibah,
>> and your land Beulah;
> for the LORD will take delight in you,
>> and your land will be married.

Today, I choose to embrace my new names, letting go of the labels I wore for so many years. They no longer fit, as God is making me a new creation. I choose to trust God in the process; He has yet to let me down.

ACKNOWLEDGEMENTS

THIS BOOK HAS BEEN A LABOR OF LOVE. Despite its brevity, much prayer and many tears have gone into it. Countless people have given of their time and energy.

Special thanks:

To the leadership and board of Alive in Christ, who allowed me to compile the material on their time and with their help,

To the participants of Alive in Christ, who were generous with their kind words and helpful feedback,

To those who read through, edited, pointed out theological ambiguities, suggested improvements or wrote endorsements: Olivia, Bryan, Heather, Carl, Big O, Russell, Pastor Jeff, and Bob,

To my designer, Rusty,

To those who heard me speak or write about the topic, even non-Christians, and were vocal in their support of its message,

To Mike Olejarz (also known as The Big O), for meeting with me on the steps of Jordan Hall back in 2000 to discuss my dreams and plans, and continuing to support me and pour life into me long after our official mentoring relationship came to an end,

To Russell, Bob, Joyce, John, Steve, and all my other unofficial mentors,

To Elizabeth, for opening my eyes to God's heart for me,

To Melissa, for the gift of friendship and pure love, and to Joe and Alicia and Jennifer and Wendy and NECFC, for opening my eyes to God's heart for everyone,

To Judy, for unending grace,

To my extended family for their support, to my dad for teaching me to aspire to goodness, to my sons for teaching me about God's heart for His children, and especially to my husband Roy, who loved me and encouraged me and put up with my doubts and fears with a smile and a cheer,

And finally, to my Lord, who gently (and sometimes not so gently) encouraged me to keep plodding on when I felt I surely lacked the strength within myself to continue. Thank You for never once leaving my side even when I thought I wanted You to, for being patient enough to tell me over and over, *Brenna, I want you to finish this book.* Thank You for being big enough to handle questions and fears and insecurities, for being faithful beyond our faithlessness (2 Timothy 2:13), and for Your example of sparing no expense in Your eternal rescue mission.

I will mention in closing that God has called me to be part of an army He is raising up. It is an army of people who are willing to fight for those who cannot fight for themselves. Alongside my passion for spiritual freedom is my passion for physical freedom—freedom for those who are in literal captivity. Thus, a tithe on the profits from this book will always go to the abolition of slavery. You can visit my website for more information:

www.livingunveiled.com

BIBLIOGRAPHY

Arterburn, Steve. *Healing is a Choice*. Nashville, TN: Thomas Nelson, 2005.

Cloud, Henry and John Townsend. *Boundaries*. Grand Rapids, MI: Zondervan, 1992.

Hamp, Bob. *Foundations of Freedom*. DVD. Produced by Gateway Church. Dallas/Fort Worth, TX: Gateway Church, 2010–2011.

-------. *Think Differently, Live Differently*. Keller, TX: Thinking Differently Press, 2010.

Levine, Robert A. *Childhood Socialization: Comparative Studies of Parenting, Learning and Educational Change*. Hong Kong: Comparative Education Research Centre, University of Hong Kong, 2003.

Mounce, William D. *Mounce Concise Greek-English Dictionary of the New Testament*. Accordance electronic ed., version 2.0. Altamonte Springs: OakTree Software, 2011.

Ortberg, John. *The Life You've Always Wanted: Spiritual Disciplines for Ordinary People*. Grand Rapids, MI: Zondervan, 2002.

Stott, John R. W., *The Letter of John: An Introduction and Commentary*. Vol. 19 of Tyndale New Testament Commentaries. IVP/Accordance electronic ed. Downers Grove: InterVarsity Press, 1988.

Swenson, Richard. *Margin*. Colorado Springs, CO: NavPress, 2004.

Thomas, Gary. *Sacred Pathways*. Grand Rapids, MI: Zondervan, 2000.

Willingham, Russell. *Breaking Free*. Downers Grove, IL: IVP Books, 1999.

Willingham, Russell. *Relational Masks*. Downers Grove, IL: IVP Books, 2004.

FOOTNOTES

1. Mounce, paragraph 4970, 4973.
2. Stott, John R. W., *The Letter of John: An Introduction and Commentary.* Vol. 19 of Tyndale New Testament Commentaries. IVP/Accordance electronic ed. Downers Grove: InterVarsity Press, 1988. pg 129.
3. These concepts are something Bob Hamp shared at the Exodus Freedom Conference in 2011. It includes my own extrapolations on hearing that teaching once and is not directly quoted.
4. This is also a concept Bob Hamp discusses.
5. Hamp, Bob. 2009. *It's Time!* [Online]. http://bobhamp.com/freedom/its-time/.
6. This example was given by Russell Willingham in the teaching, *Core Beliefs*, 2005 Exodus Freedom Conference, Ridgecrest, NC.
7. These ideas were presented by Russell Willingham in the teaching, *Core Beliefs*, 2005 Exodus Freedom Conference, Ridgecrest, NC.
8. Gary Thomas, *Sacred Pathways* (Grand Rapids, MI: Zondervan, 2000).
9. Robert A. Levine, *Childhood Socialization: Comparative Studies of Parenting, Learning and Educational Change* (Hong Kong: Comparative Education Research Centre, Hong Kong University, 2003), 93.
10. Russell Willingham, *Relational Masks* (Downers Grove, IL: IVP Books, 2004) 38.
11. I first heard this concept mentioned at a Living Waters seminar, and then at a "Healing in the Context of Community" seminar at His Mansion Ministries in NH. The extrapolation is my own.
12. This concept is taken from Richard Swenson's *Margin: Restoring Emotional, Physical, Financial, and Time Reserves to Overloaded Lives* (Colorado Springs, CO: NavPress, 2004).
13. Henry Cloud and John Townsend, *Boundaries* (Grand Rapids, MI: Zondervan, 1992), 111.
14. You can read more about default setting in my blog: http://www.livingunveiled.com.
15. This was said by Pastor Nick Fatato, currently the pastor of Common Church in Boston, MA.
16. I originally heard this story from Pastor Nick Fatato, referenced above. I did some research to confirm its truth, and also found it shared in the book *The Gift of Fear* by Gavin de Becker.
17. I originally heard this concept at physical therapy for a hip injury. It was discovered that my legs were different lengths, and what I believed to be an injury was actually a muscle adaption to the length difference. I later heard this concept confirmed by various doctors, physical therapists and chiropractors.
18. Bob Hamp, "Kingdom of God," In *Foundations of Freedom* [DVD], Produced by Gateway Church. Dallas/Fort Worth, TX: Gateway Church, 2010-2011, chapter 2.
19. In this, I am speaking of the various miracles and teachings that are recorded in the Bible, the exception being his time in the temple when He was 12 as recorded in Luke 2:46-47.
20. To read more about healthy boundary-setting, see the book reference for *Boundaries* on the Resources page.
21. Mike Haley shared this story at the Exodus Conference, 2004, during a teaching entitled *Enduring Freedom*.
22. Laura Leigh Stanlake, "Friendship or Emotional Dependency?" Teaching, Exodus Freedom Conference, 2005.
23. For a fuller explanation of how believers are God's favorite, see: http://www.livingunveiled.com.